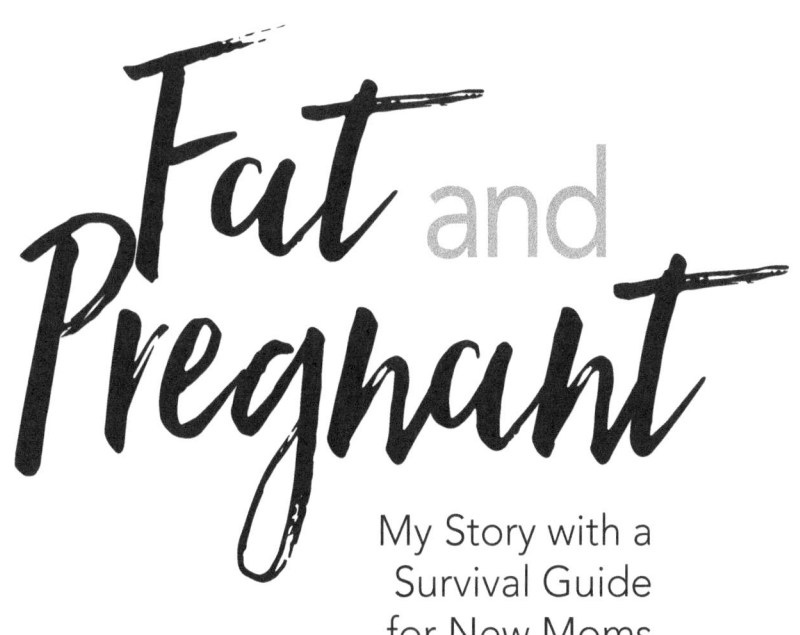

My Story with a
Survival Guide
for New Moms

Melissa Jo Graham

ISBN: 978-1-7371082-0-7 (paperback)

Copyright © 2021 by Melissa Jo Graham
All Rights Reserved.

This book or parts thereof may not be reproduced in any form, stored in a retrieval system, or transmitted in any form by any means—electronic, mechanical, photocopy, recording, or otherwise—without the written permission of the publisher, except as provided by United States of America copyright law.

Printed in the United States of America

Table of Contents

Foreword v

Introduction 1

Part One: My Story

I Met a Guy 7

Plus One 11

Waiting 13

Rejection 17

Fluffy 21

The Second Trimester 25

No Heartbeat 29

My Secret Love Affair with My Vacuum 33

39 Weeks 37

The Pain Meds 41

It's Go Time 45

It's a Boy! 49

The Fun Begins 53

Home Sweet Home 57

Part Two: Mom Survival Guide

My Pregnancy 101 .67

New Mom List 73

Breastfeeding 79

Poop and Doctor Visits 83

Birth Control and Sex 87

Working Mom 9 to 5 91

Cheat List 95

The Chapter of Firsts. 99

Get Your Body Back 103

The End is Here! 107

Foreword

For Josh,
 This story began when I met you. You have the innate ability to break down any barriers I've built up. Telling me to push through; I'm so close to the finish line. Love has many seasons; I'll take the good and bad seasons if you are beside me. Thank you for filling my cup and driving me crazy in the same breath.

To Levi and Evie,
 You bring me so much joy and happiness. I never knew what unconditional love was until I saw your faces. I look forward to watching you grow into the people you were meant to be.

To my family,
 We are all a little crazy, but you are my crazies. Without your constant support, I would never be where I am today.

To Stephanie,
 I'll never be able to put into words how grateful and honored that I get to call you sister. Thank you for being by my side as I became a mom.

Introduction

Hello! Meet me! I am Melissa the fat girl. I am the fat friend. I am always the biggest girl in the room. I've been the fat girl my entire life. I've always shopped in the big girl section. I only know sizes that begin with a two. I've been the girl that wore a size thirty. My shirts have always had an X in them—2X, 3X, or 4X. The girl too scared to try a new restaurant because I might not be able to fit in the booth. The girl that was always in the friend zone. I am the big girl.

First, you need to understand where I come from, my entire family is overweight. Everyone in my direct family has a weight problem. I grew up with everyone being overweight. Fat people were my norm. I didn't realize I was different until kids at school would point out that I was big. I was always known as the big girl with a great personality. By high school, I was sick and tired of being the best friend. I wanted to be the girl that people wanted. I was a confident big girl, but I never got the guy . . . until I met the right guy.

I realized I was worth it. I could have it all. Why was I putting limits on myself? It was a mix of both me and society setting the limits. I was led to believe that fat girls don't get it all. Fat girls will end up alone and will not have the same success as a skinny person.

Fat and Pregnant

Bullsh*t!
Blatant lies!
I found my happily ever after. Meeting Josh and becoming a mother changed my life. I got the dream. It was different from what I envisioned for myself. Did I think I could get pregnant as a fat girl? No, I always thought I would drop the weight and then have my dream life. Can I tell you what happened? Something much better.

Life didn't go as planned. Was it still great? Yes. I however struggled a lot with being pregnant as a fat girl. Honestly, the mental aspect was much harder than the physical aspects of my pregnancy. My fear of my stout fatness killing my baby debilitated my entire pregnancy. I didn't get to enjoy being pregnant. Women can hardly wait until they get pregnant. Here I was pregnant and spent the entire time worrying that my weight would kill my baby.

My views on being a fat person since I was a teenager were ungrounded. As a teenager, I felt stuck in a box and I hated being told what my limitations should be. Times have changed drastically since I was in high school. Women are breaking down walls that my younger self wouldn't believe possible. The journey into motherhood as a fat woman showed me that anything is possible. The odds were always against me, but . . . I proved them wrong. And what's more important? I proved myself wrong.

Don't put yourself in a box. Will it be easy?
No! Nothing in this world that is worthwhile will ever be easy. You could spend years thinking about what you could have done differently. Throw up the life cards and see what happens.

Part One

My Story

Fat, overweight, big girl, big bone, chubby, obese, curvy, plus size, and fatty are adjectives that have been used to describe my appearance. If you are reading this book, most likely these words have been used to describe you too. You could use these words to describe yourself or they could be how the world would describe your outward appearance.

When I envisioned my future, marriage and having a family, I would always visualize myself as a smaller Melissa. Well, the smaller never happened. I got bigger and smaller—and then bigger again—and smaller again. Josh and I got engaged but never got married. The dream version of my life never materialized.

. . . Got pregnant as a big girl.

. . . Purchased my first home as a big girl.

. . . I have accomplished everything as a fat girl.

The skinny girl life I imagined never occurred. Everything has happened while I've been overweight. I never tried to lose the weight . . . I would lose it one day. Life happens while you're dreaming of changing it. My perfect scenario never came to pass.

Whether you're proud of your fat girl status or try to hide it, I have been either one of these girls at different points in my life. I have been the one shining in my fat girl glory, never letting it interfere with my life plans. I have also been the girl that would hide because of my weight.

I wanted to write my story. The story of a fat girl that got pregnant. When I got pregnant there were no stories or representations for women that were fat and pregnant. I wanted to read stories about women that looked like me . . . there was none. I wanted a story that I could relate to. A character that I could relate to.

All the information available was for normal-sized women. All the cover pictures were of women that didn't look like me. I wanted a story for me. I wanted pictures of big girls that were pregnant. A plus-size pregnancy is different. Different is great but I didn't want to

Fat and *Pregnant*

hide because I got pregnant as a fat girl. I wanted stories that would be relevant to my pregnancy. I wanted to go to Target and see a fat pregnancy book. The book was nonexistent. My pregnancy was considered high risk because of my weight and there was no book to guide me in my plus size pregnancy.

If the sentence at the beginning of this introduction describes you, this is the book for you. This book is comprised of two parts. Part one is my big fat pregnancy story. My story was a story that I could not find anywhere else. I wanted to share exactly what happened during my pregnancy and delivery—all the details and gross stuff that we usually leave out of our stories. Hopefully, through my tears and struggles as a new mom, I will be able to help another new momma. My story is one that didn't exist . . . the story that has been mulling around in my head for years.

The second part is a survival guide for new mommas. The guidebook will give all you new mommas some direction. I have a 'Cheat List' that covers ten hot topics to help make your pregnancy and delivery smoother, and also a 'New Mom List' that covers what things you need to do to prepare for your bundle of joy. I cover some important topics like breastfeeding, going back to work, and sex.

I Met a Guy

The beginning of my story started like most other stories; I met a guy. We were young and in love. I met Josh in high school and we dated for about a year but separated before we graduated high school. We kept in touch and would eventually rekindle our relationship after about two years. We didn't move slow, we jumped in and never looked back. Before we knew it, we had moved in and I was knocked up.

We had been together for a while and were talking about long-term plans. We were working on getting our first house. We had rented for years but felt like getting a mortgage was our next step in life. Looking at houses was driving me crazy. Nothing was perfect or what we wanted. This turmoil all made sense once the pregnancy test was positive. We had talked about having children, but not straight away. It was something to only happen years down the road as we were still babies ourselves. I needed to get my ducks in a row. My ducks were not in a row. And I wanted to lose weight before having a baby. Instead, here I was pregnant and was the fattest I had ever been.

Initially, I didn't want children because of my childhood. My dad was always working, and my mom suffered from major mental health issues. He was always working because of the five kids and I always wondered

Fat and Pregnant

if the five kids are what drove my mother crazy. At the time, I did not realize that many of her actions were because of her mental issues. I didn't want to bring kids into the world and mess them up, which is how I felt much of my childhood. A lot of parents want to make sure they can give their children what they feel they have missed out on in life. I never wanted to have kids because I was too worried that I would turn out like my mom. This fear has always been a part of my entire adult life. We had talked about having kids, but it was something that we thought was far away . . . and far away became nine months.

I've always been a planner but now things were not going according to Melissa's plan. Life was going the opposite of how I thought it was going to. I was twenty-six but still felt like a kid. Now I was about to have a child and I was scared . . . I was scared because of my childhood. I was scared because I was a smoker. I was scared because I was fat and pregnant.

The main reason I wanted to write this book was because of the shame I felt during my pregnancy. The shame was a mixture of my own feelings, doctors' opinions, and society's perception of my overweight pregnancy. My plan was to lose weight, then get pregnant. I knew that losing weight would be far better for both my health and pregnancy. Any doctor would tell me to get healthy. Society would tell me that fat people don't have healthy pregnancies.

Life didn't happen that way. I got pregnant and I was still fat. I couldn't ask the baby to come back another time and wait for me to get healthier. It was too late. I didn't get to fully enjoy my pregnancy because of what other people told me could go wrong. Over the years I had this desire, and it was important for me to share my story. Even when I got pregnant the second time it was the same story all over again.

I wanted to share everything that happened in my first pregnancy—absolutely everything! I want to destigmatize the perception of being fat and pregnant. I know that a lot of things can go wrong with any pregnancy and the odds are increased when you are overweight. I wanted to share my own story because it was possible for me to have a baby.

I had no idea what to expect with an overweight pregnancy, but I figured it out. There was no how-to for big girls. One day at a time, I learned that I wasn't ruined. I realized I wasn't doomed. I realized all I could do is take it one day at a time. I created this story for all the big girls that get pregnant. This book is for you. This book is written by someone that looks like you. This is my *how to be pregnant* and *a new mom* book. I am not an expert, but I am a mom. That is ultimately a superpower, right?

This book is my full pregnancy story with some tips I learned along the way. If you're a first-time mom, welcome to the club! If you are reading this book to hear another pregnancy story, I'm glad you are here. My journey was a crazy fun ride. The unknown was scary to me. I hope my story will make your pregnancy a little less scary. I'm very excited that I get to share it with you!

Plus One

Josh was the man for me. As our relationship grew, my outlook on having a family changed. I realized that it was my choice. I could decide what type of mother I was going to be. I could choose to be different and have the family I wished to have. I could be what I wanted to be, and my screwed-up childhood didn't determine my future. It was hard for me to accept that I could be different. I felt like I didn't deserve a child that would love me. I grew up around hate and didn't believe I was capable of love. Josh taught me how to love—how to love myself and how to love someone. I wanted more with him. I wanted a life with him that included kids, growth, and growing old together. He made me want things I didn't even know I wanted. I wanted more out of life, the perfect life with him as my partner.

We were slack in our birth control measures and we got pregnant. As in, we didn't use any birth control. My period was late, but I was sure I wasn't pregnant. I wasn't sure how late because we didn't have period apps and I didn't track my period. I had taken tons of pregnancy tests and they were all negative . . . this test was positive! I immediately jumped off the toilet and ran to my sister's room (she had just moved back from Iowa) screaming like a banshee! I was unintelligible. The test must be wrong! We weren't careful, it was a real possibility we were pregnant. Could I be pregnant? I couldn't even believe the plus sign on the pregnancy test. My usual talkative self was unable to formulate words.

I had to call Josh. I couldn't wait until he got home from work. No cute gimmicky onesie for us. He didn't get a nicely wrapped pregnancy test in a box. All he was getting was a hysterical *we're pregnant* phone call. This phone call equated to a bunch of incoherent and garbled high-pitched words. He didn't even understand what I was saying. He thought the dog had gotten hit by a car! We got four different types of pregnancy tests and they all said pregnant. We even got a test that told us the results with words—no deciphering of plus or minus signs. The result of PREGNANT might as well have been on a billboard. In between the expletives racing through my head, I had a side of overwhelming fear and a glimmer of hope.

I wanted to call someone. Who do I call? Josh told me to calm down. He couldn't stay on the phone for eight hours. He had to work. I'm pregnant now, can't someone come hold my hand? I couldn't call my mom; we haven't talked in years. I had one friend that had a baby before, and I sent out a major SOS signal. Thankfully, she answered all fifty of my questions. She told me things I didn't even know to ask. First, I needed to schedule a doctor's appointment to verify the five positive pregnancy tests were positive. At the time, I didn't know the first appointment was to verify if your baby had a heartbeat.

I had no idea where to go from here. The what-ifs were on a constant loop. What if the baby wasn't alive? What if it was twins? How can I work and have a baby? Do we have enough money? I started researching overweight pregnancies on the internet. To summarize . . . don't do it! First, lose weight, then try to procreate. It's too late, Google! I'm pregnant! Tell me something good. Please, someone, tell me the odds are in my favor. Why isn't there any overweight and pregnant blog out there? I needed to find a story that was like my own story. The story didn't exist. I was embarking on a journey that I couldn't navigate with Google searches.

Waiting

The waiting was killing me. We scheduled our first doctor's appointment to verify if the pregnancy test was right. The initial shock of my results had worn off and now I was trying to formulate a plan. A plan for what? I had no idea. I needed to stay busy until I made it to the doctor. Could they tell if my baby would be healthy this early in the pregnancy? Hopefully, no alien baby was growing inside me. Did the bad habits of my adult life affect my unborn baby? I know I should have lost weight before I got pregnant. On top of my extra hundred fifty pounds, I'm a smoker. Two strikes for my first pregnancy.

    I had been smoking for ten years. As soon as I knew I was pregnant, I quit. I quit a ten-year habit within a week. I thought quitting smoking would be an impossible feat. It surprised me the most that I quit smoking. I thought losing weight would be easier than quitting nicotine. Quitting smoking was easier. I'm still battling with my eating habits. I was increasing my risks if I continued to smoke throughout my pregnancy. I didn't need a doctor to tell me that smoking was bad for the baby. I couldn't shed the extra weight, but I was able to quit smoking. Hopefully, that would be enough to get me to the delivery room.

    Do you want my quit smoking secret? I started with a small goal. I

Fat and Pregnant

wanted to quit smoking before my first doctor's appointment. I would hold the cigarette but not inhale it. I had to change my smoking routine; all my daily activities revolved around smoke breaks. Changing my routine helped me break my habit of ten years. I had withdrawal symptoms at night. Mostly night sweats and shaking. It sucked. I was miserable and shaky, but I stuck it out. The baby was my motivating factor to quit. Honestly, I had no immediate plans to quit smoking. I knew all the reasons I should quit. Everyone knows that smoking is bad, and they should quit. Knowing something is bad doesn't mean you will stop doing it.

It is possible to quit smoking. Since I quit smoking, I have been healthier and saved tons of money. While I was a smoker, I would get sick more often—especially bronchitis. I haven't had bronchitis since I stopped smoking cigarettes. My pregnancy was healthier because of my ability to have a tobacco-free pregnancy. I thought I would go back to smoking after I delivered but I didn't. Yes, I've been tempted. I knew that if I had one cigarette, I would be hooked again.

After my positive result, I noticed that my body was changing. I hoped the changes were signaling my baby was growing. The changes gave me hope. Hope that this baby would make it. Hope that I could have a healthy pregnancy as a fat girl.

My first pregnancy symptom was a heightened sense of smell. Or it could be that I was no longer a smoker and my sense of smell was restored. I could smell everything! The good and the very bad smells. It was driving me nuts! Especially, if it was an unpleasant smell. Even with the positive pregnancy test, we decided that we would continue looking for a new home. We decided to decrease our budget to prepare for having a child. My pregnancy made me an extremely unpleasant client. I was unreasonable with all the realtors we worked with during our search. Yes, I was a crazy woman who couldn't find her perfect home. The perfect home that didn't exist because I had no idea what I wanted. Pregnancy made me the most indecisive human on planet earth. We went through three realtors before we realized I was the problem, not the realtors. I never knew what I wanted. All I knew is I wanted a home that was move-in ready. I didn't need a project during my pregnancy.

We were not prepared for a house or a baby. Is any new parent ever ready? I'm a planner and this pregnancy made me less of a planner. I was in the land of the uncertain. I couldn't plan the changes that were slowly occurring. In my new normal, I let go of the reins and started to go with the flow. We were both scared to become parents. I felt like I was more scared than Josh. I was never scared about what would happen to me. I was scared of what my unhealthy body would do to my baby. It felt like so much depended on my body being able to do what it's made to do. And that made me very scared. Scared that my pregnancy would be different. Scared that we would suck as parents. We still felt like kids ourselves. Now we were going to be responsible for a human being. Responsible for a helpless baby. I still would call my dad to run big decisions by him. I couldn't call him on this news. How can I be ready to be a mom if I still call my dad?

I remembered the first time I watched a friend's newborn. The baby was crying . . . I didn't know what to do. I was clueless about what to do with a baby. I had no idea what I could do to make this baby stop crying. I was hopeful that mother nature would kick in and I would know what to do. I knew that I wanted my baby to have the best. The best of what I didn't know. I wanted my children to have more opportunities. All moms want the best for their children. All I could do was try to make the best decisions for us. Quitting smoking was my first step into motherhood—my first step at putting my child's needs in front of my own.

The days leading up to my appointment, we were extremely anxious. I wanted to get the appointment over and done with. I was becoming an emotional monster that never took a day off. Physically, my body was changing, and I couldn't stop it. I was scared and excited.

Fat and Pregnant

More scared than excited. In the dark times, I held on to hope. The hope of what could be if this pregnancy worked out. I needed answers from my doctor. I needed someone to tell me the next nine months will be a breeze. Doubtful . . . but I prayed.

Rejection

My appointment is finally here! I've never been so happy to see a gynecologist. I've had the same gynecologist for years. She was a familiar face in an unnerving time. I had my first official urine test at the doctor's office. Next, they were going to do a vaginal ultrasound to verify the results. It's not the typical ultrasound machine you see in the movies. I was in my twenties and had never had a normal ultrasound. Now I was going to have one in my vagina. I wanted the ultrasound from the movies! The ultrasound's probe looked like a long, sex toy. My initial thought was that it wasn't going to fit in me. They put a condom on the probe, lubed it up, and inserted it into my vagina. Guess it did fit!

It was uncomfortable but not painful. The screen came into focus and we saw the little blip that would be our son. He was so small! The doctor confirmed that he did have a heartbeat and was in the right place. Best news I had in weeks! A perfect moment. My doctor concluded that I was about six weeks along and I had a viable pregnancy.

We were having a baby! I was done worrying about this pregnancy. I was done coming up with new horrible scenarios. Done worrying if I would be a good mom. Done! We were ecstatic! It's official, we were going to be parents. The image on the screen told my pregnancy was

Fat and Pregnant

real. Don't screw it up, Melissa!

Then the doctor dropped the bomb. My happy bubble disappeared . . .

The doctor said they have a weight limit for their patients, and I was over it. Not five pounds over it. More like a hundred pounds over the weight limit. How could I get rejected by a doctor? What *$*#* *$# is this? Aren't doctors legally required to treat all people? How can I be too fat to come to this office? She rambled on about how my weight made my pregnancy high risk. I needed to see a high-risk doctor because they were better equipped to handle my type of pregnancy. My type of pregnancy? Now I felt like an overweight monster with a doomed pregnancy. Why didn't someone tell me this over the phone? I didn't gain this weight overnight. I've always been fat! You've seen my fat vagina for years!

I don't know when I tuned her voice out but I wasn't listening. I was over it. I was trying to hold my emotions in until we left. Suck it in! All I could think about was how fat I am. Images of my fat belly were rolling through my head. Other doctors are better prepared to handle YOUR pregnancy.

You are different. You are high risk. It "probably" won't be easy for you.

I know it wasn't going to be easy. I never thought my doctor would turn me away. She rejected me! All my worries were now amplified by her sending me to the high-risk doctor. They were unwilling to take a chance on this healthy fat girl. Yes, I'm going to call myself healthy and fat. It made me feel better in this dark moment. My happiness was gone . . . What am I going to do?

I quit smoking and was eating healthy crap! Was it for nothing? I was supposed to get good news today. Not this! The baby had a heartbeat. My baby is alive. My first appointment was not like the movies. I wanted to leave with a huge smile, instead . . . I was holding back the tears. All I felt was despair and like a damaged woman. All the worries about my weight were true. I couldn't avoid it now. She made all my fears my new reality.

I was leaving this doctor's office and never coming back—EVER.

I wanted a doctor that would handle my pregnancy whether I was fat or skinny. I honestly thought my doctor would tell me fat women have babies every day. She didn't. All she did was create new concerns for me. I cried the entire ride home. As the tears streamed down my face, I wondered what I should do next. Would the baby survive the pregnancy? Am I even made to have a baby? Is this pregnancy doomed because I'm fat?

I wanted this baby! I've heard my baby's heartbeat. This pregnancy is real. This baby is real. I wanted to believe that this pregnancy is meant to be. I wanted to believe that I could deliver this baby without any complications. I wanted someone to tell me that everything was going to work out—I wanted the fairytale version of my story.

The reality was that I was fat. I was not bloated. I didn't need to lose twenty pounds. I needed to lose an entire person. Instead, I gained a person that I'm responsible for bringing into the world. This very overweight body was responsible for growing a baby for nine months. My body had to make it nine months. Who was I kidding? My body was a walking time bomb. I couldn't drop a hundred pounds overnight. I was going to be fat and pregnant.

Fluffy

As the weeks passed, some of my fears subsided. My pregnancy symptoms gave me a glimmer of hope. I was depressed about my first doctor's appointment and was hoping the next appointment would be better. I didn't even want to go to the new doctor. I didn't want to get rejected . . . AGAIN. I didn't want to feel any worse about this pregnancy. What if we lost the baby? What if my body couldn't do this? My pregnancy felt like climbing Mt. Everest.

I took every pregnancy symptom as a good sign. I was eating healthy, sleeping all the time, and taking my vitamins. I did everything possible to make my body the best environment for a baby. The only gynecologist I ever had made me feel like a pregnant leper. My own thoughts made me feel like a pregnant leper.

After filling out the paperwork, the triage nurse took me to the back room. They took my blood pressure, weighed me, and drew some blood. The nurse asked me why I was referred to the high-risk clinic. I said, "My weight, they told me my pregnancy was high risk. They have a weight limit at their practice, and I was over that limit."

She looked up and laughed, "Honey, you might be overweight but we see women twice your size, you're just fluffy."

Fat and Pregnant

I'm fluffy!

Fluffy is great! Can I get a T-shirt made for all the fluffy girls?

I've never been so happy to hear the words fluffy. The only time I've used the word fluffy is when I described clouds. I've never used it to describe my body. I was the smallest on a scale I didn't know existed. This was probably the first and only time I was ever happy with a term to describe my fatness.

She fixed everything! She gave me hope. My nurse made me feel like an actual person instead of a freak of nature. I needed hope for this pregnancy. How many other overweight girls get sent away? How many other pregnant fat girls felt doomed? I'm not the only one. There will be plenty more ahead of me.

My new doctor discussed my pregnancy and asked questions about me. She told me about the possible complications and that my weight could impact my pregnancy. She didn't lie to me. She told me there was no point worrying about my weight now. I didn't need to lose weight now. My focus was a healthy pregnancy. My goal was to make it to the second trimester. If I could make it to the second trimester my risk of miscarriage would decrease significantly. We didn't run out and tell our family. We were still scared of not making it to the delivery room. I was worried about disappointing myself. I couldn't disappoint other people if I lost the baby. So, our lips were sealed.

I hated cooking food during my pregnancy. I detested the sight of food. I don't remember cooking during my pregnancy. I am not sure what I ate every day. Thankfully, Josh cooked for me and the baby. The baby was controlling my appetite. I ate differently once I was pregnant. I still ate a lot of food; it was just in smaller portions. I was unable to eat large amounts of food. I could only eat small meals. I would even try to eat like I did before I was pregnant. It made me miserable. It would make me feel super bloated and nauseous. What worked well for me was eating small meals and snacking throughout the day. No weird pickle cravings. No sweet cravings. I wanted to eat meat!

Fluffy

The most unexpected thing about my pregnancy was that I lost weight during my pregnancy. I lost weight until the last few weeks of pregnancy. How is it possible that the only time I lost weight was when I got knocked up? Most women would be thrilled. Oh, and was I thrilled! I figured my pregnancy would make it okay to gain some weight. It felt like my pregnancy was destined to be different.

The nurse told me that some overweight women don't gain weight during pregnancy. What? Was it possible that I don't become as huge as I envisioned? I never thought I would be dropping pounds. Winning! The pounds kept on coming off. Don't get me wrong, I was still eating. I was just eating differently than I usually did. I have been fat my entire life. I was a fat kid. I was probably a fat baby too. The fact that I was losing weight when I wasn't even trying . . . mind-blowing! Until I was pregnant, I didn't realize how I got fat. Yes, I'm a fat person that didn't realize how she got fat. I didn't get fat overnight. I slowly gained weight. It sounds crazy but I've always been a big girl. I never realized how dysfunctional my relationship with food has been my entire life.

Healthy foods and portion control did not exist in my present life or childhood. My upbringing greatly influenced my eating habits. I ate heavily processed food and almost zero healthy food. If it wasn't what I was eating, it was how much I was eating. I wasn't mindful of my eating. I wasn't eating perfectly during my pregnancy but I was trying to make better decisions.

I made better choices. I was pregnant and didn't have time to tackle my relationship with food. It's hard enough to be pregnant. My body was constantly changing and my taste for food was different. My pregnancy was not what you see on the TV screen. I wanted to crave pickles! Why did my pregnancy have to be different? Was it different because I was fat? Or was it just me? I wanted to see someone that looked like me and was pregnant. I wanted to read a story that was like my pregnancy . . . And the only person that told me I was normal was a nurse.

Fat and Pregnant

Fluffy suddenly became a triumphant term to describe. I never thought I would be happy to be described as fluffy. I was thrilled! I needed some positivity in my life. The fluffy label made me feel like I had a fighting chance. My fluffiness could keep my baby alive. I know it sounds crazy . . . it gave me hope.

The Second Trimester

If I had to pick a favorite pregnancy trimester it was the second trimester! I had more energy and wasn't sleeping all the time. Finally, I was enjoying being pregnant. I was starting to feel like a normal pregnant lady. I wasn't having any issues. I felt good. I started to see the end of my pregnancy.

I loved being pregnant! Was this even possible? I was ready to show my pregnancy bump. No bump here! No one could tell that I was pregnant because I was fat. I looked fat! I was ready for strangers to ask when the baby was due. I'm fat. I'm pregnant and I wanted a special badge or VIP parking. When was that going to happen . . .? I was ready to display my bump to the world.

Talk about body image issues. Pregnancy changed the way I looked at my body. My body was changing every day. No one on the outside could see the changes. I felt all the pregnancy changes. I was pregnant but no one could tell. I consider myself a confident big girl. I've spent much of my life hiding my stomach. I never wore tight clothes because of my weight. I wore clothes to hide my stomach. I wanted the opposite when I was pregnant, I wanted to show my baby bump off. It made me feel insecure. My belly was just a fat belly; not a pregnant belly.

Fat and Pregnant

I wanted to show my pregnancy stomach on full display! There was a baby inside. I too wanted to wear the cute clothes.
   I was never able to find cute plus size pregnancy clothes. Plus size pregnancy clothes were unobtainable and not stylish. They had no good options for me. I was crushed. My dreams of being a cute fat pregnant girl were over. I didn't have the maternity shoot where I looked like a pregnant goddess. Even if I could find cute clothes, they weren't comfortable. I wanted comfort. Tight clothes were not my friend during pregnancy. The only maternity store with a plus size section had about ten options. Most of the clothes were made for my Grandma! My maternity photoshoot never happened. I didn't feel pretty the entire pregnancy and didn't want pictures immortalizing my unhappiness.
   I ended up wearing my normal clothes. I would stretch the clothes out to make them work for my growing belly. Plus size maternity clothes are getting better but not cheaper. Not all pregnant women want to look like they are wearing a sheet as a maternity dress. We want stylish clothes! Time to design cool clothes for fat, pregnant women! Big girls desire cute clothes too! Advice: *buy for comfort.* Comfortable clothes, shoes, bra's, and granny panties!
   My gender reveal appointment was finally here! I wanted to know. We had picked out names and we thought we were having a boy first. I eagerly pulled my shirt up and let the tech squirt jelly on my belly. The waiting was killing me! Before she would tell us anything, she had to take all the measurements. Hurry up, lady! We want to know if we are having one baby or two babies. Is it a boy or girl? She had to press hard on my belly to get a better image of the baby. She kept pressing but she couldn't see the gender. Mercifully, he had all his fingers and toes.
   The baby finally moved, and she was able to see what we were having. It's a boy! She showed us his penis. A boy! She was pointing at the area—and this told us it's a boy. The area looked like a blur. You say it's a boy . . . We believe you. I was ecstatic the baby was moving.
   We felt this was a great time to call everyone we knew. We couldn't

wait to call all of our family. I was sick of keeping my pregnancy a secret. I wanted to shout it out to the world! We had waited to tell anyone because I was so scared I was going to lose the baby. My family and friends were suspicious because I wasn't smoking or drinking. We got our first picture of our son. What a moment. Our first proud parent moment!

Everything was going great. I was still hesitant about being too hopeful. There was always a possibility of something going wrong. The doctor told me our baby was measuring on the high end of the scale. His size was above average and could increase my risk of complications during delivery. I was beginning to think that no matter what I did every appointment was going to end like this. They were going to tell me that my results equaled some possibility of him not making it out.

I felt that it was never enough. I couldn't have a happy moment without someone reminding me that I was fat and pregnant. I was doing everything possible to make it to the delivery room. What if I did everything possible and I still lost my son? I followed all the pregnancy rules. Stop reminding me that something could go wrong. I hoped that my pregnancy would go against the normal statistics for overweight pregnancies. I knew my odds; I knew it's a near impossibility to have zero complications with any pregnancy or delivery. Let me believe that I can be different.

I hoped that I could. . .

No Heartbeat

My belly was getting hard and round. It was a physical sign that only I could see. To everyone else—I simply looked like a big girl. I promise, I'm not just fat—I do have a baby inside this belly! It seemed like time was speeding up. My pregnancy was starting to feel and look real. We had the baby shower and got to celebrate our new baby with our friends and family. We decided on a theme for his room and worked on getting the room ready for his arrival. Everything seemed to be falling into place. It felt official once he had a room in the house. We put the crib, car seat, stroller, and various baby gadgets together. I was beginning to feel like a new mom. We had no idea how to use half the baby items. It was a major milestone to have all the baby items ready and the room prepped for our new baby.

The first kick was magical! Melissa fact: *it took longer to feel the kick because I was fat.* In my expert opinion, he had to get big enough for me to feel it through my extra layers. At first, the baby kicks felt like gas. How could I mistake a kick for gas? My belly was stretching every day. It was an awesome sight! Slightly freaky . . . but awesome to see the life growing inside your belly. All the kicks and movement reassured me that everything was going well with my pregnancy. The kicks

Fat and Pregnant

and growing belly were a physical reminder that I'm growing a human being. Once the kicking started, it didn't stop. I loved every minute of the kicks.

At my next appointment, everything changed. It was a routine appointment that almost crushed my world. How could things change so quickly? The high-risk clinic rotated the doctors during my routine appointments. This way I got to meet all the doctors at the practice. The doctors became familiar with my pregnancy. I'm not sure if this is the standard or what happened during my pregnancy.

It was a routine appointment . . . that almost killed my dreams of being a mom. The nurse was having difficulty finding my baby's heartbeat on the machine. She couldn't find the heartbeat. All I could hear was the sound of the machine. The sound of nothing. Another doctor came into the room to try and get a heartbeat. Nothing. He tried again. Nothing. They tried a different machine.

Nothing . . .

Just silence.

Was he alive? Was the machine broken? Why am I alone? I couldn't remember the last time I felt a kick. When was it? Why don't I remember? I'm the worst . . .

Now I was facing this, alone.

I thought this would be like every other appointment. I wanted to go back to the ordinary appointments. I wanted someone to tell me my pregnancy was boring. They were sending me to the ultrasound clinic. It was only about five minutes from the doctor's office. The longest five minutes of my life. I couldn't even articulate words because I was in such shock. All the fears from the beginning of pregnancy were coming true. I've killed my baby.

I had to pull it together. No tears. I didn't cry on the drive to the clinic. How was this possible? I was completely numb. Nothing could have prepared me for what they were going to say to me. Whenever a doctor's office tells you to remain calm, the opposite is what happens.

Now I was freaking out. I didn't even know what to say.

They said there was a good chance the baby didn't make it.

What?! He cannot be dead. I just had the baby shower. I've washed all the new clothes. His room was ready. That room was made for him. The bed was for him. NOOOOO! My baby wasn't dead. I felt like I was dying inside.

It's my fault. Why did I get pregnant while I was fat? I should have waited. My baby deserved a chance. The doctors told me I would have complications. I was fine with the complications if it hurt me. I didn't care what happened to me. I didn't believe that I would get this far and lose him. I thought everything would work out. He was real! I felt him move inside. He knew I was his mom. Why couldn't he move right now? Maybe he was sleeping? Give me a sign!

Maybe my fat was preventing them from picking up the heartbeat. My doctor had called ahead to prepare the clinic. The technician started to tell me this kind of thing happens all the time. You are overweight; sometimes the baby doesn't make it.

WHAT!!!!

Suddenly, everything I had been dreading was becoming my reality. This was normal because you had gestational diabetes and high blood pressure.

Wait! I did not have those. You got the wrong patient. Wrong pregnant lady. The only medical condition I have was being obese. I'm not running marathons or drinking green juices, but I've had a healthy pregnancy. I can be a healthy fat girl, right? I've never eaten this healthy in my entire life. Was it not enough? I couldn't press rewind and lose a hundred pounds. It's too late for me to lose the weight. Dude, just tell me if my baby has a heartbeat or not.

He squirted the gel onto my belly. I saw my baby boy on the monitor. Then . . . I heard the sweet hum of his heartbeat. I knew it! The best noise I've heard in my life. The technician's face said it all. He was shocked. He was convinced the baby was dead.

Fat and Pregnant

He's alive. He was fine. He was moving. He said he had a very strong heartbeat. I finally let out a sigh of relief. His heart was still beating. He wasn't dead. Breathe Melissa . . . breathe. The technician brought a doctor in and they both were surprised by his heartbeat. I could tell by their reactions. I didn't care about the details.

He was alive!

Melissa snapped back to reality. The doctor reminded me that my baby was going to be a big baby. Based on his measurements they were estimating he would be a ten-pound baby. How would a ten-pound baby get out of my vagina? I mean, how does any size baby get out? But a ten-pound baby? My mom had five children and all of us were big babies except one. How did she deliver five babies? My youngest sister was almost eleven pounds. What was I getting myself into?

I didn't care that he was a huge baby or what would happen to me. My baby was alive! He wasn't stillborn. Even if the delivery was horrible, it didn't matter. I wanted him to make it to the delivery room. My emotions were roaring, and I needed to get out of this doctor's office.

I was angry.

I was relieved.

I blamed the doctors for this ordeal I had to go through. At the time, they put me through this emotional rollercoaster. I knew my fatness got in the way of their heart monitor. They made me feel like my baby was dead. I was another fat girl statistic to them. I'm a person, a unique individual—not a statistic. I was a mom. Even if he was still growing inside of me, I was still a mom. You would not take this away from me. I was sticking with anger at this point. It prevented me from crying my eyes out. This was MY baby. He was going to make it. And I will make it. I will deliver a healthy baby—as a fat woman. Hear my fat girl voice ROAR!!!

My Secret Love Affair with My Vacuum

I've survived the worst doctor's appointment of my life. Honestly, I wanted to forget that day forever. Nothing in this pregnancy was certain. I knew I could still lose him. The appointment was a reminder that life isn't guaranteed for my son. I was writing down every time he kicked. My baby kick radar was on full alert. I was glad that he was still kicking and moving all the time. My easy pregnancy was starting to feel more uncomfortable.

Get ready! I thought I peed a lot at the beginning of my pregnancy. As I neared the end, I was best friends with my toilet. I never stopped peeing. It was a vicious cycle of drinking tons of water and then running to the bathroom. I even started going to the bathroom through the night. Once the baby drops it feels like a bowling ball in your uterus. Tons of pressure down below! The pressure will not go away until the baby is out.

Nesting was the most classical pregnancy cliché I fully experienced. My need for a clean house quickly escalated. Everything needed to be clean. I've never been a clean freak. My sister calls it organized chaos. My old vacuum did not meet my pregnancy standards. I had to have the latest and greatest vacuum available. The floors had to look

Fat and Pregnant

impeccable. My days were full of waddling and cleaning the house. My vacuum was my new best friend. No cleaning lady would ever be able to meet my pregnancy cleaning standards.

I worked full-time until it became unbearable. I slowly reduced my work hours because it hurt to move. Everyday activities were slow and painful. Overall, I still felt like my pregnancy was going smoothly. I hated slowing down, but I needed to take it easy. I had to do everything in my power to get him into the world safely. I was enjoying prepping our home for our baby. Who doesn't like to decorate? I was stocked with everything baby-related. I had stuff that I didn't even know how to use. Trust your fellow moms, they know how to make your life easier.

The only thing that made me less miserable was the recliner. I never owned a recliner until I was pregnant. It was the only way that made sleeping bearable. If I laid on the bed, Josh would have to pull me up. So, I avoided laying down.

I finally got my pregnancy belly. I had to wait until the eighth month to get my belly. Finally . . . when people asked when I was due, I could say that I was pregnant. Before when people would ask—I was just the fat girl. They asked me so many times if I was expecting. All the big girls reading this book know exactly what I am talking about.

I was proud of the weight I had lost and of my big belly. Does that make sense? A fat girl being proud that her belly is expanding? No! I gained a couple of pounds at the end of my pregnancy. It wasn't much. I still weighed less than I did before I got pregnant. I loved my pregnancy belly glory! The big belly was getting in the way. If I dropped anything, I couldn't pick it up. It was impossible to bend down. I mean . . . I couldn't even see my feet!

The word I would use to describe my third trimester would be uncomfortable! I was physically uncomfortable and nothing I wore made me comfortable. You're uncomfortable and running to the bathroom twenty-four seven. I voluntarily signed up for this?

I enjoyed the slowness of the last weeks of my pregnancy. It was the last few weeks of freedom before I became a parent. I slept a lot. I needed it—I was about to be seriously sleep-deprived. I wish I worried less at the beginning of my pregnancy. The worrying made me miss out on the joys of pregnancy. I was so worried about what society would think of a fat pregnant mom. How my weight would affect my baby and my child as they grew older. The unknowns made me a crazy person. I was always expecting something to go wrong. I knew it could happen at any moment. I was so close. I just needed to make it a little bit longer.

I tried to enjoy the last few moments of my pregnancy. I felt if I let the happiness in, it would be snatched away from me. When the doctor said my baby had no heartbeat, it was my everything I feared becoming my reality. I didn't get close with my baby because maybe it would hurt less if he didn't make it. Melissa, don't get attached to the baby growing inside you. Make sure he makes it out alive. Miscarriages happen all the time. The odds were increased for me to have a stillborn baby because of my high-risk pregnancy. I kept my new motherly joy at arm's length. The worst-case scenarios were still a real possibility until I delivered. If I could get him in my arms, then everything would be okay. A million things could still go wrong. Maybe it won't. Maybe we can make it.

I can do this!

39 Weeks

It's delivery time! The doctor's birth plan was to induce me at thirty-nine weeks. My master plan was to have a natural delivery. My weight made my delivery risky. The doctors had two concerns: the baby's size and this was my first pregnancy. He was estimated to be around ten pounds, his size was high on the growth charts. The doctors worried if I would be able to deliver a baby that size. Heck, I was worried too. Could I deliver a baby that big? The first delivery is always difficult. The next deliveries will be easier. Now you tell me! I figured my body would know what to do. My body has never done this before, give me a break. I can deliver this baby. It will be easy, right? My body will do what it is meant to do because my brain was thinking about delivering a baby the size of a watermelon.

I would never make it in the medical field. It freaks me out. I'm scared and amazed at what a human body can do. I did not research anything about childbirth before giving birth. I didn't ask other moms for the scoop on delivery. I didn't want to know. I was scared to have information about delivery. It was easier not knowing. Knowing would make me worry and come up with hundred plausible scenarios. I decided to go with the flow instead of researching childbirth. It took a lot to get my baby in this world safely. The doctors and nurses do this every day. We are the visiting team.

Fat and Pregnant

It was a perfectly choreographed labor routine that I was ignorant about. My childbirth crew was Josh and my sister Stephanie. I was the lucky one of my sisters to get to experience childbirth first. Why couldn't they get knocked up before me? Since I was the oldest sister, I got to wear the labor and delivery badge first. At least, I would get to torment one of my sisters during my labor. Being the older sister has its advantages.

I was oddly calm throughout my pregnancy considering that everything and the medical world told me an overweight pregnancy was doomed. I didn't worry about what could happen to me because I would risk my life to ensure my baby survived. I've made it this far . . . we were so close now! If you had asked me nine months ago, I didn't believe I would make it to the delivery room. My mom superpowers were finally kicking in. Can you visualize my super mom cape? All moms have super mom powers in the delivery room. The unknown wasn't going to scare me. I was ready to rock this delivery!

Disclaimer: The next few chapters are the raw and unedited story of my first pregnancy. There is no way to make labor politically correct. Labor is extremely gross and beautiful at the same time. It changed my life. I had no idea what to expect in the delivery room. I didn't have a personal guide to walk me through this journey. I was on my own. I was waiting for my inner goddess to take over now. I needed to find my inner warrior. This was the moment I started to regret I didn't read every pregnancy book available on planet earth. Too late, Melissa . . .

Time to get naked! I was ready to rock the sexy hospital gown. If you are worried about showing skin, get over it now. Everyone will see your vagina! I was so worried about everyone seeing me naked. Once the contractions started, you will not care who sees you naked.

Once they got my IV set up, I was relieved. The worst was over, right? Next, they put a heart rate monitor on my belly. It would monitor his heart rate during my labor. The monitor was attached to a very large Velcro strap. The heart rate monitor wasn't made for a girl my size. It kept sliding off my belly. It was made for a normal size pregnancy belly.

Not for a fat pregnant girl. I spent so many hours cussing at the heart monitor. It was uncomfortable and made me sweat.

    The doctors were ready to induce my labor. I never had Braxton hick's contractions and any active signs of labor. My body didn't know magically that now was go time. Pitocin is a medicine they gave me to speed up labor by helping my uterus contract. It didn't take long before the medicine kicked in and I felt my first contraction. The pain was not what I had envisioned. I was already miserable. Now I was uncomfortable and in pain. I don't know what I expected contractions to feel like—maybe like a bad leg cramp. It did not feel like a leg cramp! I had pain in my back, legs, and stomach. The contractions were increasing in frequency and in pain level. They suddenly became unbearable. Once I had the Pitocin, the pain didn't slow down.

    Hours passed without me getting any closer to having a baby. All I felt was pain. In the wee hours of the morning, the doctor told me my labor wasn't progressing. So, the magical medicine in the IV bag wasn't working? Nope. The contractions never stopped, they just didn't progress. The doctor told me it was time to break my water. Wait . . . you can do that? The doctor described breaking my water as an easy procedure. She explained it like all doctors do, it will be super quick. They do it every day. Easy for her, not for me.

    The doctor sat on the bed beside me. I thought we were going to talk about breaking my water. Until she pulled out the foot-long gloves. How do gloves this long even exist? Am I a horse? The gloves went past her elbows! Was my vagina a bottomless hole? She used a tool that pinched my bottomless hole. I felt an immediate release of pressure.

    Finally, I was in labor. I thought so . . .

    During the entire procedure, Josh was sleeping. Stephanie was trying to comfort me. It wasn't working. I don't know if I was more traumatized by the procedure or the gloves. I couldn't process what just happened because the sound of Josh's snoring was pissing me off. Wake up buddy! It took me screaming or my sister screaming. Who knows? If I was not sleeping, he was also not going to sleep.

The pain has officially started. I experienced my first intense contraction and it sucked. I wish I could make it stop! I already missed my easy contractions. The easy part was behind me. The intensity and frequency of my contractions kept increasing.

This was the real deal.

The doctor had to monitor the baby's heartbeat because the external heart rate monitor kept falling off. What's next? An internal heart rate monitor was inserted into my vagina. Yes. Why would this shock me? What other medical procedures or tools were in my future? I didn't even know this existed until I had one inside me. You want weird? The monitor is sticking to your baby's head. Yes, the monitor was stuck on his head, dangling from your vagina. It was beyond freaky.

In between the dangling heart monitor and my increasing pain, I was running to the bathroom every five minutes. It was already a process for a fat pregnant butt to go to the bathroom. I already had the pregnant waddle down. Now I was in my hospital gown with a metal rod hanging down and an IV bag in tow. It didn't stop. Why could I not stop peeing? I was sick of getting up and down.

My bathroom trips were going great until the billionth trip to the bathroom. This time the internal heart monitor fell on the hospital floor. My doctor had zero tricks left for monitoring my baby's heartbeat. She got a new heart monitor and reattached it to his head.

When was the finale? I felt like my first labor experience wasn't going as planned. I wanted it to be a piece of cake. Honestly, I was hoping the baby would fly out. My dreams of an easy pregnancy weren't in my future. I had planned not to have an epidural. I thought I could handle the contractions. I thought I had a high pain tolerance. My high tolerance became nonexistent once the contractions got closer together. My birth plan was thrown out of the window. The pain was manageable until my water broke.

Get me the drugs. I'm ready for the epidural.

The Pain Meds

Where is the medicine man? I've had enough. I was lashing out at everyone because the pain was getting worse. I was hoping the epidural would at least make the pain bearable. Wasn't the epidural the magic medicine to make childbirth bearable? I needed relief, ASAP. I was scared to get an epidural, but the pain made me a willing patient. I was at the point that I would try any medicine to make it stop.

My white knight was here! Once the anesthesiologist walked in, I knew the pain would go away. I had to sit up for him to work his magic. I had to bend over the edge of the bed while a nurse kept me from falling off the bed. A nurse that weighed about a hundred pounds was holding me in my plus-size glory. How was she doing this? I was triple her size. Don't drop me, please!

The epidural felt like a cold thread being threaded through my back. The epidural didn't hurt but was cold as hell. I was trying to remain calm and not freak out. Josh was curious about the epidural process. The doctor quickly shut down his dreams of watching the epidural. It's a hospital procedure and you could faint watching it. Josh wasn't focused on keeping me calm. He wanted to watch the show. I couldn't believe I survived my first epidural.

Fat and Pregnant

My labor crew increased by one person. Josh was adamant about his mom being at the delivery. I love his mom. I was afraid she would see me at my worst. This was the worst pain of my life and I wanted to scream obscenities. I was holding back because Sharon was in the room. I was naked and I didn't want her to see my goodies. I didn't want her to see my vagina! I didn't want to look at my own vagina. She saw my tattoos. Sharon would think I am a tramp! A tramp giving birth to her grandson. I'm not sure why I got stuck on who was in the room. I was the only one that couldn't leave.

I felt like a horrible person for wanting her gone. I wanted her to see the delivery of her grandchild. But I didn't want her to see me naked or falling apart. I was crumbling. My tough girl act was nonexistent. I wanted to cry. I felt like I was holding back because she was in the room. She had five kids; she knew the deal. This was my first child and I can't handle it.

Yes, I was a crazy woman! I was so hyper-focused on his mom being in the room that the nurse took notice. She could tell it bothered me. She didn't ask questions. She didn't judge me. My hero wore scrubs. New rule, Sharon had to go once I was fully dilated.

Initially, I felt good after getting the epidural. The honeymoon had to end. The epidural took the edge off, but the side effects started. My body temperature was switching between hot and cold. I also got a case of extreme itchiness. I was itching like crazy, but I had no rash. Yes, the doctor told me about the side effects. Was I really listening? No, I just wanted the pain to stop.

The constant temperature changes were driving me crazy. I would have a hot flash and have to strip down and get soaked in wet rags. Then I would have a cold flash, and everyone would layer me with blankets. It was back and forth between the two temperature extremes.

The pain was getting worse, not better. Did he give me the wrong stuff? The whole reason I got the epidural was to make labor easier not worse. Or was I having a reaction?

The Pain Meds

As my labor progressed, I didn't care who was in the room. I didn't care about the weird side effects. I wanted to be at the finish line. As the contractions grew closer, the nurse routinely checked to see how far I was dilated. The only thing that felt different from twelve hours earlier was the pressure I felt in my back and vagina.

I felt worse.

Screw the damn epidural. It didn't work for me. I was beginning to understand the full meaning of the word exhausted. I had no food or sleep in over twenty-four hours. I had zero appetite. I was in too much pain to fall asleep. The last thing I cared about was food. At this point, I didn't want to be pregnant anymore. I would do anything to speed this up. The reality was that I was not in control of how fast this baby comes out. I wanted to hold my baby so this would all be worth it.

Pressure = the baby was coming.

Yes, the feeling of pressure was a good thing. This was music to my ears. The nurse told me it would feel like the biggest poop of my life. Basically, when you feel like you're going to sh*! in your pants, the baby is coming. Got it! Now I have measured my poop level to a room of people. I could have never imagined a nurse telling me this was the next step. Ladies, don't be surprised if you're asked to measure your poop in your pants level.

I felt like I was in the clear because I was ready to poop. The doctors ruined my happy moment. They let us know that some of my vitals were beginning to concern them. The baby's heartbeat was increasing, and I had a fever. My body wasn't responding well. The doctor's plan: Tylenol and IV antibiotics. What was my initial reaction? To freak out. I've had zero medicine this entire pregnancy. I had a drug-free pregnancy. I didn't want the drugs. This was my clean pregnancy.

It took a lot of persuading for me to take the medicine. I couldn't make a rational decision. I had to trust the doctors and my family. It could have been the exhaustion or the pain. I couldn't make any decision on my own. What if these were other side effects from the

Fat and Pregnant

epidural? Josh was able to snap me back into reality while addressing my concerns. Ultimately, I would do what was best for my baby.

I started to worry about the safety of my delivery. I wasn't dilating fast enough and now I was having complications. Once they started talking about C-section plans, I started to pray for a safe delivery. I had a million thoughts running through my head. Mostly that this was proof why this fat girl shouldn't have got pregnant.

I decided to do whatever the doctors wanted me to do. I wanted to get this baby out, I had to give over control. I never really had control; I had the illusion of control. I had to remain calm and follow orders. Soldier Melissa, reporting for delivery. I waited for the medicines to kick in. The Tylenol knocked the fever out and I started to feel less doom and gloom.

Things changed quickly after my fever broke. I started to feel more of everything.

More pain.

More pressure.

More I'm going to sh*! in front of everyone.

Everything was hurting. I paged the nurse. This must be the real deal. She checked and I was fully dilated. We were about to have a baby. I was going to be a mom. I was scared and excited at the same time. It was time.

Wait . . . Where was Josh?

It's Go Time

I was in full labor. All kinds of people were getting paged and called into my room. Doctors and nurses were running in and out. I was watching the flurry of activity surrounding me. My only job was to remain calm. In my head, I was in full panic mode. Physically, I was in the worst pain of my life. Mentally, I was trying not to panic. The nurse gave me my last dose of the pain medicine before it was time to push. It's time to push.

The last dose of medicine only numbed my legs. It didn't numb my vagina. My vagina felt like it was ripping apart. Why didn't the epidural numb all the labor pains? Why was the epidural numbing the wrong area? I felt the pain everywhere else. The only pain-free area was my legs. If I wanted to run out of the room, I would fall flat on my face. My legs were dead weight.

Stephanie and Josh were holding my legs up until my sister couldn't handle the dead weight. Could I blame her? I wouldn't want to hold my own legs up. My nurse took over the leg-holding duty. Everything was a blur by this point. I looked at my door and there was an audience of doctors. A full audience for this fat girl's delivery. Have you never seen a fat girl give birth? I don't know when I stopped caring about who

Fat and Pregnant

saw me naked. But I did stop caring. I didn't care who saw my vagina. Everyone can look! There were only two doctors with front row tickets to the Melissa's Vagina show.

Josh's mom never got kicked out. Once the viewing party arrived, she got stuck in the corner. Sharon didn't move a muscle. She was worried that if she moved someone would kick her out. I didn't care that she had seen everything. I felt depleted and could use everyone's strength to help me reach the end. I needed her support.

All the movies show the breathing technique which I didn't practice. Honestly, I thought it was a load of crap. As I gasped for breath, I realized I should have mastered breathing during childbirth. I didn't know how to control my breath. I was being told to control my breathing. I wasn't even sure if I was breathing.

I was dominating child labor like a pro. I kept pushing and pushing. My baby was slowly coming out. Inch by inch, I was getting closer to meeting my baby. I knew childbirth was a long process, but this was taking forever. I wasn't sure how much longer I could keep on pushing in these small increments.

I kept on pushing. And pushing. I did not feel like I was getting any closer to seeing my son. I was screaming obscenities at everyone. I was out of breath. I can only imagine the craziness I was spouting from my mouth. I know they weren't nice words. I wanted this to be over and done with. I wanted to run away. I couldn't feel my legs, running wasn't an option for me. Could I have a five-minute break?

I've never fainted. I felt like I was going to faint. I had nothing left in me. I couldn't push anymore. I was not a tough cookie, I was losing my mind. I was giving up. Let's do the C-section. I didn't even care that everyone was seeing me give up. I had nothing left.

What do I remember about this moment? The random doctor telling me to stop screaming. She was a member of the audience. The audience doesn't talk to the leading lady! You are not part of the show. You aren't helping to deliver my baby. I wanted to smack this lady. I will never forget her face. Who did she think she was? She told me I was wasting my energy. She had a valid point. I was wasting my energy by screaming. I wanted to yell; it made me feel better.

Josh yelled, "Every time you stop pushing the baby gets sucked back up!"

Wait.

I've been pushing for an eternity and I'm not closer to seeing my son. I wanted to cry my eyes out. I thought he was slowly coming out. Every time I stopped pushing his head would go back up my vagina. I couldn't believe it. I should have watched a childbirth video. Nope! All this pushing was for nothing. He was getting sucked back up when I stopped pushing. He needed to come out, not go back up.

Twenty-four hours and still no baby. Just a pissed-off and exhausted pregnant woman. Would it be easier for me to have a C-section? I mustered up the last bit of courage I had left and pushed. I kept pushing. When I felt like giving up, I would push further. I pushed with all the remaining energy I had left in my being. He was out!

I did it!

I've never felt so much joy. Joy that he was out. Joy that I was done pushing. I was on the verge of quitting. I didn't quit. The last push was the hardest thing I've ever done. This journey was all worth it when I saw my baby. I survived.

The delivery room pushed me to my physical and mental limits. Right past my limit I found the silver lining. My baby was on the other side. When I felt like giving up, I pushed harder. I didn't think I could do it. I didn't believe in myself. I found the courage in myself. Everyone in the room was cheering me on. They couldn't push the baby out for me. It was up to me. I can do anything; I am a mother.

It's a Boy!

Once he was out, I physically felt better. The pressure I felt was gone. I did it! This fat girl had a baby! They laid him on my chest with his umbilical cord still attached. I was excited because I finally got to hold my baby. He was covered in blood and gunk. He was perfect. Josh got the honor of cutting the umbilical cord. I've never felt so many emotions in a twenty-four-hour period. My feeling of exhaustion disappeared and now all I felt was pure joy.

A pediatrician gave him a full checkup. I was relieved that he was breathing and had all his fingers and toes. I did it! I brought him into this world while I was a fat girl. I wasn't another statistic. The last nine months were full of obstacles and I survived. Looking into his eyes made it all worth it. Once I looked into his eyes, I knew he was mine. I knew I was meant to be his mom.

Television gave me a skewed version of childbirth. The media portrayed childbirth as super easy or the impossible. I didn't watch the childbirth YouTube videos. I never watched the videos to prepare for what I experienced in the delivery room. I preferred to be in the dark on all delivery-related matters. If I read all the books and watched all the YouTube videos it was nothing compared to this real-life experience.

Fat and Pregnant

No movie, book, or doctor could have prepared me for what I felt like when I delivered my son.

It was not easy.

It was hard.

It was gross.

It changed everything.

My delivery story is not over. I've delivered a baby, but I still had work to do. They still needed to clean me out. Everyone else was busy taking pictures of Levi. The doctors were discussing the afterbirth plan with me. Wait, what is the afterbirth?

Beware, squeamish readers! I'm about to give you the real low down on what happened next. The end scene is upon us! The afterbirth process—I'm glad I never researched. I thought I was done with childbirth. The doctor had to push the placenta out.

It wasn't pretty. It was disgusting and hurt like Hell.

They pushed hard on my stomach. They pushed from different angles. There has to be a method to the madness, all I felt was pain. I thought I was done with pushing. Now, I felt like my innards were being pushed around.

When was this going to stop? Then it stopped. I felt a big release of pressure. The contents of my placenta flew out. They missed the bucket. There was blood everywhere. The poor doctor was front and center to the blood fest. When I looked up again, he was covered in my blood. His clothes were drenched in my bodily fluids. My blood had splattered across the room. It was everywhere.

It was on the doctor's shoes, the walls, and the bed. Everyone was acting like it was completely normal. How was I not dead? Then I saw the amount of blood in the bucket. Josh and Stephanie told me it smelled like death. I don't remember the smell. Once the afterbirth was out, I felt better. I felt like the old Melissa.

I survived delivery and the after-birth process. The doctor informed me that I have torn my vagina. It wasn't bad enough that I pooped in front of twenty people. Now I've ripped my vagina. It didn't make me feel better that vaginal tears were normal. My vagina was a battle zone that I didn't want to see. It took a couple of stitches and I was back to normal. After what I've survived, a vaginal tear was the least of my worries.

I wanted to share every detail of my childbirth. Pregnancy and childbirth showed me the powerhouse that is in every woman. You will have your own unique story. I learned that I was now part of an amazing group of women. My body went through a lot—mentally and physically. The medical aspect of childbirth still astonishes me. My fat pregnancy made me wonder if I would make it to the delivery room. I learned that I was a powerhouse.

I wouldn't have survived without the awesome doctors and nurses. It's a daily routine for the doctors and nurses. They helped me through the entire process. They knew what I needed. Trust me, ladies, I wanted to give up. They gave me words of encouragement that helped me push through. Everyone in the labor room lifted me up when I thought I had nothing left.

The fact that I made it to the delivery room was a major accomplishment. I never took it for granted. I didn't believe I would be able to carry a baby based on the statistics for big girls. The entire experience was pure magic. I remember every detail of my delivery, it felt like time slowed down. I wanted to cherish being able to bring a life into this world. The odds were stacked against my pregnancy and I made it.

I finally got to see my son all cleaned up. This was the moment I've been waiting for since I saw the plus sign on the pregnancy test. I looked into his beautiful eyes and held his small hands.

Speechless.

I was not prepared for the instant love I felt when I saw my son. Holding my tiny human for the first time. My heart was full. I survived the most exhausting, painful, and rewarding experience of my life. I made it!

Fat and Pregnant

I looked at every part of Levi. I wanted to remember how he looked in this moment. How it felt, how he smelled, and how he looked at me. I was meant to be his mother. The pictures from this moment painted a completely different picture. I remember the elation and joy. In the pictures, my face was swollen, and I looked like I was hit by a truck. Stephanie tried to fix my hair. She couldn't fix me; I was a hot mess.

My pictures were raw, but it was the proof that I survived childbirth. I was not the mom with the fresh makeup and blowout for birth pictures. I was simply a woman that went through one of the craziest experiences of my life. I was in awe of the new life that I had created. The picture represented the beginning of my life as a mother. Every time I see the picture, all the warm fuzzy feelings come back.

I made it.

The Fun Begins

Did I leave you with a warm fuzzy feeling? I probably grossed you out! I delivered a baby . . . Now I have to keep him alive. I don't know how to take care of a baby. Finally, I got to hold him for a while. I got to have my new mom moment. Let me indulge in my new mom bliss.

Once I started doing an inventory of myself, I realized I was hungry. Feed me! My first meal as a mom was hospital food. A cold turkey and cheese sandwich that tasted fabulous! The nurse told me to slow down. She was worried about me throwing up. I wanted more food. I can handle it!

Once I got cleaned up, I felt like a normal human being again. I took a couple of ibuprofens for the pain and was moved to a new room. I was ready to get out of the bloody room. The room was not bigger or better. My new nurses introduced themselves and gave me a crash course in having a newborn. I was hoping for a nap. Instead, I got my marching orders as a new mom.

Every two hours I would try to breastfeed. Oh yeah, I was the source of his food. So, what you're telling me is that my night of rest doesn't exist? I didn't even know how to breastfeed. They would send a lactation nurse to show me how to breastfeed. The nurse showed me

Fat and Pregnant

the basics of breastfeeding to get me through the night. The reality of motherhood was sinking in. As all my family started to leave, I realized it was me and Josh. Oh, and our baby.

My body has gone through so many changes. It was not over yet. Bring the granny panties to the hospital. A lot of women swear by mesh underwear. They didn't have them in my size. Trust me . . . sexy panties don't exist after having a baby. The last thing I cared about was feeling sexy.

Get ready for the mother of all periods. I bled the most I've ever bled in my life. It felt like I was bleeding to death. It got worse before it got better. I had a baby, I should get a break from being a woman for at least a week, right?

At first, every time I walked, I would bleed through the pads, underpads, panties, and clothes. A blood trail would follow me everywhere I walked. I was wearing the largest pads ever invented plus an underpad. I would still bleed through it all. I couldn't slow it down. All I could do was to survive it.

I'm going to share a heartwarming story that will remain with me until I'm old and gray. I knew Josh was a keeper because he helped me when I was at my worst. Josh had already seen all kinds of disgusting things during childbirth. The blood wouldn't stop coming. No matter how many layers of protection I would put on, it didn't matter. It would almost fly out of me. Josh acted like it wasn't a big deal. He would follow me and clean up my blood trail. I didn't have to ask him, he did it without hesitation.

I was at my worst and it didn't matter. I had a supportive partner that was with me through the good and bad. I didn't even know that I would need him in this way. I was already missing the period-free months. Now I was experiencing the payback.

The crash course in motherhood was already overwhelming me. I had no idea what I was doing. It was day one, and I already felt like a bad mom. How was that even possible? Some things came natural and others felt foreign to me. There was so much we didn't know about parenthood. What I thought about babies, didn't apply. I thought nature would take over and I would be a perfect mom. I wasn't. I had to learn along the way.

We were NEWBIES! We had no idea how to do anything. The nurses knew it. Did we have *newbie* written in invisible ink on our foreheads? Somehow, we survived our first night as parents. We made it to lunch before we put our white flag up. Levi started to cry, and we didn't know what to do. I tried to feed him, and I changed his diaper. He wouldn't stop crying. What should we do? We didn't know.

We paged for help.

The nurse came in—a.k.a. our savior came in for the save. She knew! The way she looked at us said it all, this is your first baby. Yes, we are clueless. She said, "It's time for a crash course in baby." She gave me the most valuable information we received as new parents. She said new babies will need one of three things. She told us to go through them until our baby is content.

THE 3'S OF BABY

1. Hunger – Feed the baby!
2. Burp – Time to burp!
3. Diaper – Change the diaper!

So, she proceeded to show us the correct way to change a diaper and how to swaddle a baby. I was never able to master swaddling. My son did not like the feeling of being swaddled. After she explained what we should do, we felt a sense of relief. We could handle three things, right? It was a blessing that we were still at the hospital and had help. Our time was running out, we had to go home soon. Then we were responsible for keeping him alive.

Fat and Pregnant

We knew the basics and became parents along the way. We tried not to get overwhelmed by being new parents. I was still in sleep deprivation mode and trying to survive—in between the visitors and new parenting.

You are not alone. So many parents will go through the new baby phase. There are so many of you that will not know what to do. Don't expect perfection. You will learn and figure out how to be a mom.

It was a huge accomplishment to survive childbirth. Now I was in the newborn war zone. We were both learning how to be in this world. I was mostly learning how to keep him fed and happy. I was beginning to realize the lack of sleep I could expect for the foreseeable future. If I survived twenty-four hours of labor, then I could survive to taking the baby home, right?

I will survive.

I'm a great mom.

Positive words will help, right?

Home Sweet Home

I'm going to be brutally honest; I was terrified to leave. I was going to miss my nurse team. I loved pressing the button and someone coming to my aid. Can I take a nurse home? We were going to have to do this on our own. I wasn't ready. I was getting into a routine with my son after the journey to Hell and back. But we could not stay in the secure comfort of the hospital forever. It was time to put on my fat girl panties and brave the next step . . . and that was going home.

The hospital required us to have the car seat inspected. Josh brought the car seat to our hospital room. The safety technician showed us how to buckle Levi into the seat properly. We had no clue how to secure him in the car seat. We read the manual and we were still clueless. This time there was a real baby to put in the seat. Who knew we would be learning so many things at the hospital? But we had a home that was awaiting us. The car seat technician had to verify that the base was installed correctly. Oops . . . It was installed backwards. He gave us a quick lesson in car seat safety and proper installation. Thankfully, this technician position existed at my hospital. I know we aren't the only clueless parents out there.

As we drove away from the hospital, we headed straight towards our new life as parents. We had the typical slow ride home from the

Fat and Pregnant

hospital. Like all new parents, we were worried about waking Levi up. What if he started crying in the car? I had so many irrational fears as a new mom. Your baby will cry in the car. You will figure it out. Yes, I had a major fear of my son crying on the way home.

I was looking forward to catching up on sleep. Looking back, I was insane to think sleep was a possibility with a newborn. New moms only dream about sleep. Hopefully, I will get more sleep than I did at the hospital. Once I got home, I will be able to relax. Yes, the word 'relax' came out of my mouth. Did I think I was on my way to the spa?

At the hospital, it was a revolving door of doctors, nurses, and visitors. Now I was in control of my environment, I could set my own pace. I would be able to set my own schedule instead of conforming to the hospital schedule. Guess what? I got home and it didn't get better. I didn't know what sleep deprivation felt like until I became a mother. I could never catch up on sleep. It was extremely hard to get into a routine. A magical routine that I believed would make everything better . . . It didn't exist. I was struggling to find my sanity as a mom. If you find the sanity or the spa treatment, please let me know!

It was nice to be at home. We had tons of help when we got home from the hospital. Our family knew we were newbies and were trying to help when possible. We had a lot of visitors that wanted to meet our new edition. Under normal circumstances, I love seeing people. Visits are great during normal times. Let's be real, I was in survival mode. I was sleep-deprived, bleeding everywhere, and recovering.

Try to limit the visits. I got very overwhelmed with all the visitors. I worried about the house being cleaned. What was I thinking? It didn't matter! No one should judge the cleanliness of your home when you have a newborn. If they do, they can leave. This was my first lesson in trying to be a perfect mom. I wanted to appear to have it together. I was barely holding it together. I believed that my job was to do it all. To be perfect.

It was all an illusion. I was my harshest critic. I thought I could do it all on my own. Your family and friends should be bringing you food.

They should be cleaning the house while they visit. Not judging. News flash! It was not going well. I was tired and barely found the time to shower. I learned quickly how to operate and function with no sleep. I was learning how to push through even though I was exhausted. I fell in love with being a mom.

I was learning how to be a mom.

The nights were the roughest. I was supposed to sleep at night. This didn't happen for a long time. I learned how to be a somewhat awake mom that was excellent on autopilot. I kept doing the Threes of Baby until he was happy. It worked for me. What helped me through the nights? Buffy the Vampire Slayer was my best friend. The love triangle of Buffy, Angel, and Spike kept me company.

Advice I wish I could go back and give myself. Be patient with yourself and your baby. Don't rush motherhood and expect perfection. You will struggle as a new mom. You and the baby are learning this new world together. Take it one day at a time. It will take time to adjust to your new normal. Life doesn't magically click when you get home. I struggled to find normalcy. It helped to set up healthy boundaries with visitors. You and the baby are the main priority. Everyone else can wait.

Fat and Pregnant

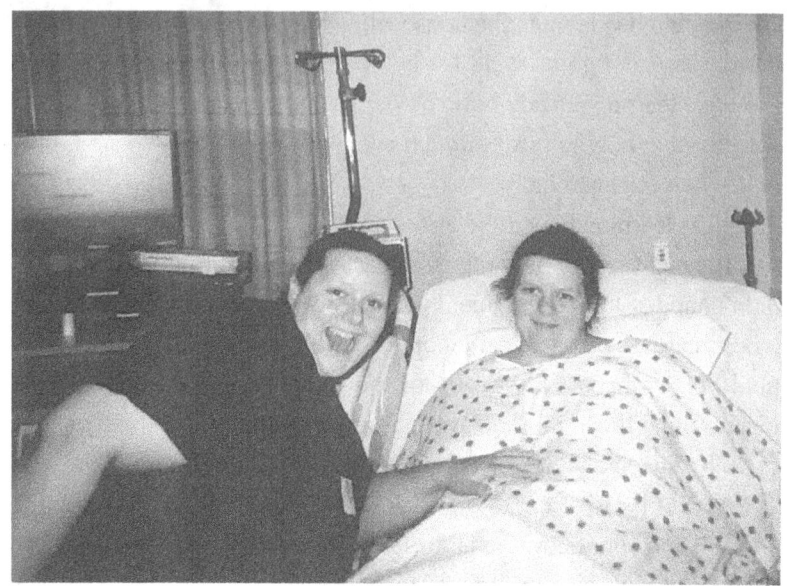
Me and Stephanie

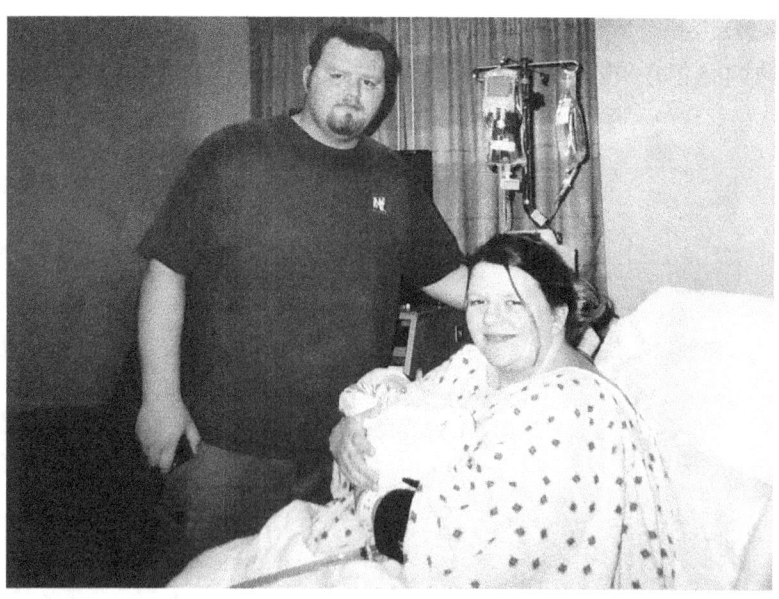
Our first picture as parents

Home Sweet Home

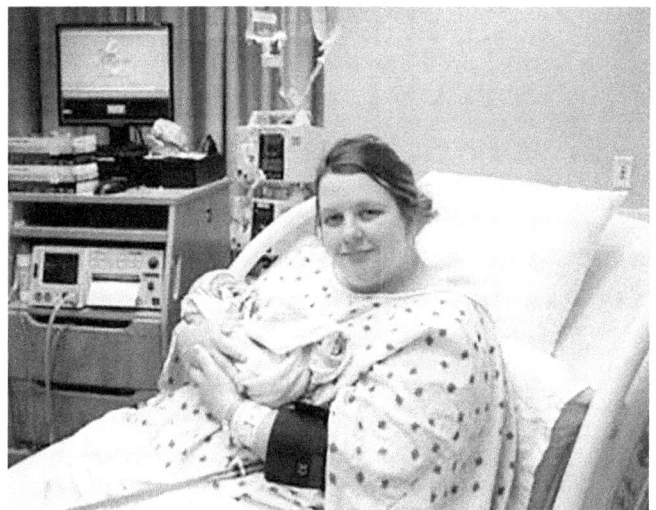
I did it, I'm a Mom.

Part Two

Mom Survival Guide

We made it through my fat pregnancy and delivery! This section of the book is a guide to motherhood seen through my eyes. This is the guide I wish I had as a new mom. I am no medical expert but have a ton of real-life experience. I am a new mom that has survived my first pregnancy and first kid. In this section, I'm sharing a couple of tips, lists, and stories to make your first pregnancy easier. This is Melissa's guide to survive your pregnancy, delivery, and bringing a newborn home.

I hope this guide will help you along your journey. I have undergone a huge learning curve during my pregnancy and bringing baby home. My major mommy fails will make it easier for you. They will also remind you that you are not alone in mommy fails. I couldn't get over how many things I was clueless about when I brought my son home. Believe it or not, you will figure it out! It's amazing what your body can do throughout your pregnancy and delivery. Trust me, I still can't believe I did it as a fat pregnant girl. It was easy to make a baby. Everything after the baby-making was difficult.

Hopefully, the next chapters will be full of the information you didn't even know you needed. There are so many things I wish I knew when I was a new mom. All these little things made a huge difference in my day-to-day new mom existence. I know you will find something in the upcoming pages that will make your transition into motherhood smoother. Welcome to the Mom tribe. We are in this together!

My Pregnancy 101

You're pregnant . . . now, what do you do? There are so many unknowns about pregnancy. Are you ready for a deeper look into my pregnancy? When I first found out I was pregnant, all I could see were the things I couldn't have anymore. That was followed by all the weird things that happened to my body. The joys of becoming a mom.

> **WHAT NOT TO EAT/DRINK WHILE PREGNANT:**
> - Deli meats
> - Certain imported cheeses
> - Different types of seafood
> - Caffeine—I miss you Starbucks!
> - Raw eggs
> - Unpasteurized milk
> - No alcohol. Sorry Ladies!

I avoided the items on this list to the extreme. I was lucky to be pregnant and didn't want to take any chances. My only goal was to make it to the delivery room. I avoided anything that would be risky for my pregnancy. I gave up some of my favorite foods during pregnancy. How I love Mexican queso and chips. No queso at the Mexican restaurant!! I didn't eat it. My baby wanted the queso! After I delivered, I found out that queso is mostly American cheese and I could have been eating it all along. Why didn't I research Mexican queso, WHY?!

Hangry

Honestly, I had no idea what I wanted to eat, ever. The baby was controlling my decisions. At least, that is what I told everyone. I never knew what I wanted to eat until I was starving and beyond reasoning. Get prepared because pregnancy hunger will make you a crazy monster. Your hubby should prepare for an alien to inhibit your body and to never be satisfied. Snack often. If you get hangry, you will become a monster and your relationship might not survive it. Make sure your hubby has your favorite pregnancy foods on standby.

Cravings

You always hear about the crazy pregnancy cravings. I was told I would crave pickles and chocolate. I don't even like pickles. Now, I'm going to suddenly crave pickles because I'm pregnant? I never craved the pickles. I craved meat and potatoes. Nothing about my pregnancy was typical. I craved meat. Who on earth craves meat during pregnancy? This weirdo did. Sweet foods or sugary drinks disgusted me. I never was a water drinker until I was pregnant. I drank a ton of water.

Food Aversions

I avoided so many foods! I made a lot of food decisions based on my sense of smell. Most smells made me feel nauseous. My aversion to foods reached its peak in my second trimester. I never knew what I wanted to eat. Just the sight of raw meat or the thought about cooking my food made me nauseous. Josh would do most of the cooking. Only if I could figure out what I wanted to eat. How did Josh survive my pregnancy food cravings and aversions? He realized the baby was a little monster making me a crazy woman. He learned how to navigate my crazy cravings and not bring any foods into the house that would make me nauseous.

Morning Sickness

Don't hate me for this! I never had morning sickness. I have no idea why, but I never got sick. Yes, I was extremely lucky and I knew it. I have no tips or secrets to share. My sister-in-law was pregnant three times and she had morning sickness with all her pregnancies. I empathize with any mom reading this book that has experienced morning sickness. Focus on the fact that morning sickness is only a short-lived symptom of pregnancy.

Boobies

The first physical change was my boobs. They were HUGE! Like huge watermelons. Like where did these big guys come from? I never had large boobies—now I felt like they were going to hit me in the face. My big girls did however not last long! After I stopped breastfeeding, they deflated. My boobs never returned to their pre-pregnancy perkiness.

Vaginal Discharge and Peeing

I missed the memo on this one. No one told me how thirsty you will be while pregnant. Get ready. Your thirst will be impossible to quench. Guess what? Your increased intake of water will make you a regular visitor to the bathroom. Get ready to pee all the time. Use the bathroom before you leave the house! Expect to use the bathroom everywhere you go. The more pregnant I got, the more trips to the bathroom.

Buy panty liners! No, you will not get through the entire nine months without wearing a feminine pad. Near the end of your pregnancy, you will have accidents. Ladies . . . get ready to pee in your pants. I want to warn you, be prepared. How can you prepare to pee in your pants? You cannot prepare to pee in your pants. Will you pee in your pants? It's very likely. You will not be the first pregnant woman to pee on herself. Be prepared to leak if you sneeze or laugh.

Bad news, there are two reasons to buy panty liners. Another top-secret pregnancy symptom is increased vaginal discharge. I wasn't expecting excess vaginal discharge. Why is my body doing all this weird stuff? Today's lesson—buy the panty liners. It will either rescue you from peeing on yourself or from the discharge. I'm classifying this under the crappy parts of being pregnant.

Indigestion

I never had a problem until I was pregnant. Once there was a baby growing inside me, everything gave me indigestion. Have TUMS on standby. Sometimes just looking at food would give me ingestion issues. Melissa's secret remedy for indigestion—milkshakes. Seriously, they make it go away! If you have indigestion, go get a milkshake.

Sex

Sex is different. Different, in a very good way. Pregnancy sex was great! Some of the best sex of my life. Pregnant sex was more intense than normal sex. It was easier for me to orgasm while I was pregnant. Crazy, right? We had sex until the very end of my pregnancy. The last few weeks of my pregnancy, sex was extremely uncomfortable. It was difficult to find a comfortable sex position. Once I was feeling the baby move, it made having sex weird. Josh thought that his penis was hitting the baby. I never worried about his penis touching the baby's head. I got freaked out if I felt the baby move during sex. What calmed my anxiety about sex? I pretended the baby was sleeping while we were doing the deed. You wouldn't even believe how many conversations we had about the baby being aware that we were having sex. It was heartening to find humor in my sex anxiety.

It Gets Hot

I was always hot. I never sweated until I was pregnant. I can't believe how much I sweated during my pregnancy. Thankfully, I wasn't pregnant during the summer. I would have been naked the entire time. The air conditioner was never cold enough for my hot flashes. I got really sick and tired of being hot and uncomfortable. I wish I could hang out in an industrial freezer.

Crazy Dreams

Your dreams are not a safe zone. My thoughts were already running rampant with worrying. My dreams were very dramatic, and my nightmares were horrifying. Mostly, my dreams involved aliens. Alien babies, invasions, and alien gunfights. Get ready for the craziest and weirdest dreams.

New Mom List

> **MELISSA'S TOP THREE MUST-HAVE ITEMS**
> - Sleeping Machine
> - Bouncy Seat or Swing
> - Bottle Brush and Drying Stand

Create a Registry at Amazon, Target, and Walmart

I am partial to Target because who doesn't love Target? They gave me a new mom goodie bag. Who doesn't love free stuff? A Target rep gave me the scan gun and let me loose in the baby section. Create your baby registry online. I was old school and wanted to use the scan gun—even though I had no idea what to scan. I felt like I scanned everything in the baby section. My sister worked in a daycare, so she was able to tell me what I needed to buy. I scanned diapers, onesies, pacifiers, breast pumps, wipes, and blankets. I was pregnant before Amazon was the giant it is today. Now you can have baby necessities delivered to your doorstep. Add the major ticket items to your registry. Most people will give you newborn clothes and diapers. You will always need diapers. Lesson: if possible, register at all the major retailers. It gives your friends and family the opportunity to purchase from their favorite store.

Coupons, Coupons, and More Coupons

Register your baby at formula and diaper companies. Disclaimer, I am not saying to not breastfeed. I am saying, be prepared. I thought I would be able to breastfeed. I had no contingency plan. There came a day that I couldn't produce milk and my son was hungry. My saving grace was a small sample of formula the hospital gave me. Always a backup plan. Have a contingency plan if you are unable to breastfeed or decide you don't want to breastfeed. I had major issues with breastfeeding. I tried and breastfeeding didn't work out for me. It doesn't matter what brand you use; you will spend big dollars on formula. The average price for a can of formula is seventeen to twenty-six dollars. The biggest expense other than formula will be diapers, wipes, and clothes. When you can, print or digitally load coupons. Download your favorite retailers' apps to see specials and coupons on your regular purchases. Buy in bulk when the items go on sale. We had a stockpile of the most used items (diapers and wipes). If couponing isn't your thing, save on subscription services. Save when and where you can because baby expenses add up quickly.

Buy Used Clothing

Shop for used clothing on eBay, Facebook marketplace, and search for clothes at yard sales. This is where you can save tons of money. This was a strange concept to me. I wanted my baby to have only new clothes. Used is better and will save you money. They grow extremely fast in the first year of life. All the newborn clothes will not last long. You can find a lot of quality, used baby clothes from other moms. When I had my second child, I bought used clothes, store-brand diapers, and re-used a lot of baby items from my first baby.

Sleep Machine

The best purchase I ever made was a music machine/night light. Stop reading this book and go buy one on Amazon or Target. Why are you still reading this book, go buy it! My son was a light sleeper. He would wake up whenever he would hear a sound. It drove me bonkers. The sleep machine saved my sanity. This is my top recommendation if your baby is a light sleeper. It was one of the only reasons he would sleep throughout the night. (You might be haunted by baby music in your sleep.)

2x Diaper Pads

Buy a minimum of two diaper changing pad covers for the diaper table. You will need it. Trust me! When you have a messy diaper on the cover you can remove the dirty one and have a clean one ready to go. They are inexpensive and will keep you prepared for a messy diaper duty. It will take you only one night after an upset tummy to see the real value in two diaper table covers.

Nipple Pads/Nipple Guards

Nipple guards helped protect my nipples and reduced nipple soreness. Your boobs will be sore, but the guards will help to reduce the pain. The nipple pads also helped with leaky boobs.

Coffee/Caffeine

I started my relationship with coffee after having my first baby. I became a Starbucks Gold member when I had a newborn. Coffee kept me caffeinated throughout the rough days. What was life like before my coffee addiction? I don't remember it. The first few weeks, you will be on autopilot. Whatever your caffeine poison is—have it on standby. I'm not recommending a caffeine addiction, but it can help when you're sleep-deprived.

Purchase Baby Laundry Detergent

I started with Dreft detergent because everyone told me this was the go-to baby detergent. Honestly, I didn't know babies required special detergent. Dreft detergent worked great for my first child. My second child had very sensitive skin and I had to use sensitive baby products (Honest and Seventh Generation).

Buy a Baby Swing/Bouncy Seat

The vibration and movement helped calm my son. The bouncy seat and swing will help keep your baby occupied while you're doing things around the house.

Baby Proof the House

Make sure you baby proof the house before you bring your baby home. Prepare while you are not in survival mode. Babies are little explorers and baby proofing is essential to prevent injuries. You will quickly realize how many things around your house are dangerous for your baby. My advice: go baby proof your house!

Purchase a First Aid Supply Kit

Make sure it includes nail cutters and a booger sucker. The booger sucker will save you! F.Y.I., your baby cannot blow their own nose. Hopefully, they won't get sick and won't have to use it. Also, spend the money on a good thermometer. When they are running a temperature, you will want results fast.

Pacifier

I was determined to be a mom that didn't use a pacifier. It didn't last long. I tried a pacifier, and it was a tool that helped this mom. The pacifier helped soothe him and helped him fall asleep.

Sign Up for a Parenting and CPR Class

I wish I took both classes, but I didn't. Most pediatricians offer parenting classes for free. I had no idea that they offered parenting classes. The CPR class is inexpensive and an invaluable resource. My daughter is a walking choking hazard. She has almost choked on more occasions than I can count. Get the training, it's worth it!

Diaper Bag

Spend the money on a quality diaper bag. The diaper bag will basically turn into a diaper bag and purse combo. Your bag needs to be stylish and functional. One of the best mom hacks: always pack extra wipes, diapers, clothes, and bottles. Your baby will eventually spit up or poop on their clothes.

Contact Info

Have your pediatrician's information handy. When you're a new mom, a lot of scary things happen. The unknowns will be scary. You cannot prepare for all the things that will happen to your child. When my son had his first fever, I freaked out. I had no idea what to do. The doctor's office will be the first line of defense and the best friend you did not know you need. They guided me through the fevers, cuts, upset stomachs, and sicknesses. We were lost parents when we went home with our son. Take comfort in that we had no idea what we were doing. We survived; you

Fat and Pregnant

will make it too! Most pediatrician's offices will have a 24-hour hotline that you can call a nurse. Trust me, this service will become your new best friend. I called them more times than I would care to admit. They gave me helpful tips, calmed my fears, and provided priceless medical advice. Call the nurse line and Google less.

Breastfeeding

Spoiler alert. I wanted to be a breastfeeding mom. Breastfeeding didn't work out for me. I naively thought breastfeeding would be easy. I thought I would be a natural at breastfeeding. I failed horribly. I had issues with feeding positions or getting my son to latch on. I felt like I was suffocating him with my huge boobs. I was his energy source, and now I couldn't provide him food. Breastfeeding was physically painful, and I always felt I was doing it wrong. My emotions were constantly fluctuating, and this added to my new mom inadequacy feelings.

I struggled with milk production and figuring out how to breastfeed. We saw a lactation specialist and the doctors would offer advice. None of it was working. Why didn't my boobs work? Levi wasn't gaining weight. Instead, he was losing weight. The doctors started to worry if he was getting enough nutrition. How was I already failing at being a mom? The one thing he needed from me; I was unable to do. I started to supplement the breast milk with formula. He had to put on weight, or we were in trouble. We even tried blessed thistle, massaging my breasts, and using the breast pump. Nothing we tried helped with my milk production.

I felt like a HUGE failure. I couldn't even feed my own baby. Women had been doing this for hundreds of years, but I couldn't master it. I was unable to provide him with food. What was wrong with me? I was willing to try anything.

But it was too late, he preferred formula.

I was never a breastfeeding expert. But I so hoped I would be a breastfeeding rock star. I wanted to share a couple of things I learned as a brief breastfeeding momma. I picked up a few useful facts along the way.

Soreness

Your boobs and nipples will be sore. Nipple guards helped me at first but not for long. Since I never mastered breastfeeding, I never got to the pain-free part of breastfeeding. Toughen up buttercup, you have a long road ahead of you!

Leakage

Your boobs will leak. Make sure you try to empty out your boobs with each feeding. If your baby is full, make sure to pump the milk out for later.

Energy

Breastfeeding will drain the energy out of you. Your battery will already be low—focus on resting and eating. You will be sleep-deprived and milk production will make it worse. After each feeding, I would feel extremely depleted.

Eat

You will need to eat. I was initially worried about eating too much because I wasn't pregnant anymore. I didn't want to gain the weight I lost while pregnant. Baby is out, this was the time to lose the baby weight. I was in survival mode and I was not focused on my eating habits. I was eating junk and it didn't give me the energy I needed to feed a baby. My crappy diet affected my milk production and energy levels. I would skip meals because I was worried about gaining weight.

Positions

Breastfeeding positions do matter! Nurses gave me the best advice. I was not a natural at breastfeeding and was willing to take anyone's advice. I kept on trying to move my breast around Levi's face. Every position I tried, it felt like I was suffocating him with my breast. The nurse told me to move the baby, not my breast. Simple advice that worked. Move the baby into the position. Find what position works for you and baby. It's essential for you to be comfortable and relaxed—it will help you be a successful breastfeeding Mom.

My attempt to breastfeed was over. It was hard to let go of this part of motherhood. I tried to get my breast milk to come through, but I failed. My baby was happier when he drank formula. And I was happier that he was drinking formula. I could not ignore the positive signs of using formula.

It's one of the biggest regrets I had about being a new mom. I wondered about all the things I could have done better. At the time, I had to do what was best for my baby. I had to trust that I was making the best decision for him. I couldn't live up to the ideal that I created for myself. My vision of pregnancy, delivery, and motherhood was not my reality. I created this Mom ideal and then hated myself when I didn't live up to it. I wasn't a bad mom because I couldn't breastfeed. There are plenty of formula-fed babies that are healthy children. My baby was fed and happy. And that was all that mattered. In the end, I fed him—although not in the way I had planned to.

Breastfeeding Story

I wanted to share a funny but very real story about my adventures with breastfeeding on the go. We were on the way to a doctor's appointment that was about thirty minutes away. We were about twenty minutes into our drive when my son started screaming. We stopped at Burger King to see why he was crying. I owned a not-baby-friendly Nissan Sentra that had zero room to maneuver. Josh went inside to get us breakfast while I learned my first lesson in mothering on the go. Visualize a plus-size woman shoved into the back of a small car—breastfeeding with my boob out with a croissant sandwich in my mouth. This is not what I pictured would happen when I became a mom. Were you hoping for a more glamorous image of motherhood? Get used to the non-glamourous life. Motherhood is not what you see on television or social media. It will be much better—and your own special story.

Poop and Doctor Visits

Get ready to talk about poop, A LOT! One of the things I learned quickly was the art of describing your child's poop. Every time you go to a doctor's appointment, it's poop talk. Oh, the poop will change a lot with a newborn. Keep track of the number of diapers and the type of poop. You will track the poop and it gets extremely smelly. How does such gross stuff come out of such a beautiful baby? Wait until your baby is eating baby food, then the deadly poop begins.

I was surprised by the number of routine doctor appointments in the first year. You will follow an appointment schedule based on your baby's age. Eventually, the appointments will decrease to yearly appointments. Get ready to be a routine visitor at your pediatrician's office. They will closely monitor your baby's growth throughout the first year and offer helpful advice.

Fat and *Pregnant*

Here is a quick cheat sheet on your routine appointments.

THE AMERICAN ACADEMY OF PEDIATRICS RECOMMENDS THE FOLLOWING WELL-CHILD SCHEDULE:

1 Week	Weight, feeding, and jaundice check. Newborn vaccines if needed.
2 Week	Weight check and physical exam. Newborn vaccines if needed.
1 Month	Weight check and physical exam. Newborn vaccines if needed.
2 Months	Physical exam, growth and development. Any vaccines if needed.
4 Months	Physical exam, growth and development. Any vaccines if needed.
6 Months	Physical exam, growth and development. Any vaccines if needed.
9 Months	Physical exam, growth and development. Fingerstick to test hemoglobin levels. Any vaccines if needed.
12 Months	Physical exam, growth and development. If needed tuberculosis skin test. Any vaccines if needed.
15 Months	Physical exam, growth and development. Any vaccines if needed.
18 Months	Physical exam, growth and development. Any vaccines if needed.

These appointments were a reminder of how much my baby was growing. I was always amazed at the growth chart printouts. I miss the onesies and clean diaper smell. Your pediatrician will have tons of resources for you. Take advantage of them! You can never be over-prepared for a baby. Trust me, I wish I was more prepared. Motherhood is a battlefield . . . at least, it felt like one.

Birth Control and Sex

Let's talk about having sex after having a baby. Are you ready to learn about sex after birthing a watermelon out of your vagina? This is the chapter that you are either looking forward to or avoiding. Sex was one of the last things I was thinking about after having a baby. Eventually, I was ready to have intercourse. I waited until I was ready emotionally and physically for my sex life as a mom.

Create your own timetable for intimacy after childbirth. Depending on your recovery time, it might take a long time before you're back in the bedroom. The recovery time is different between natural and cesarean delivery. You are the only one that can decide when the right time is for you. It's possible that you could be healed physically but not mentally ready for sex. Be patient with yourself, sex will happen when you are ready. Don't rush intimacy.

Before delivery, the doctors reviewed the different birth control options that were available. I was indecisive about which options I wanted to use after the baby. I knew I didn't want another baby anytime soon. I wanted to make the best decision for my new life as a mother. My only experience with birth control was taking the pill. The birth control pills I tried had negative side effects for me. They weren't the right birth control option for me. I didn't want to try another pill to only have negative side effects again. I wanted to try something different, a more permanent birth control measure. I tried the Paragard IUD. I went with an IUD because it lasted five years and I didn't have to remember to take a pill.

Birth control options are an extremely personal decision. My only advice would be to research all the options and speak with your doctor. Your doctor will be able to advise you on what will work best for you. I always had trouble remembering to take the pill. I didn't want to risk forgetting to take the pill because I was a new mom. I wanted to focus on keeping my baby alive! There are plenty of options, don't give up. If you don't want to use birth control, stay out of the bedroom!

Since we are done talking about birth control, I want to discuss sex after a baby. I wondered if I would even want sex after having a baby. Would my sex drive be non-existent? Eventually, I did want to have sex. Was it immediate? NO! I had to get my MOJO back.

Physically, I had to give my body time to heal. My vagina ripped during childbirth. What if I had sex and my vagina ripped again? I would never want to have sex again. I was scared to poop because it felt like my stitches were ripping. I didn't want to make it worse by having sex too early. The doctor gave me the stamp of approval to be intimate, but I wasn't ready to do the deed. Would I ever feel the same about sex or myself? Would I feel the same towards him? Does my vagina even look the same?

It took me longer to get past what happened in my vagina than it did for Josh. He saw me at my worst and still found me sexy. I had to handle my own insecurities concerning my new sex life. My emotions were out of control and I was not being patient with myself. It took time to get my sexy back! Sex happened naturally for us. It wasn't intimidating. I was fearful about being open with Josh. I'm a mom now. Will he still want me? Can I be sexy as a mom? All my fears were nonexistent once we actually did the deed.

I hope you have the right person at home. Having a patient partner is crucial to any relationship. A partner that doesn't rush you to have sex after delivering a baby. Josh has been a real partner through a lot of good and bad seasons. We have been together since high school and have seen a lot of changes throughout the years. Having a baby was one of the biggest events in our lives. We grew together as people and now we were becoming parents together. Having someone that is patient and understanding is essential to sexual health after childbirth. As new parents, you will find your rhythm in the bedroom.

Your sex life will be different. A different sex life is okay. This is a new chapter in your life. Will you feel like your twenty-year-old self? No. One day you will feel normalish. You're a mom now, accept your new grown-up sex life.

Mom Truth

Sex with kids. You will be extremely lucky if you can finish before the baby cries . . . or a kid knocks on the door. Fun times!

Working Mom 9 to 5

Work, work. Maternity leave will eventually end. The days of watching every moment of your baby grow will end. You will have to go back to the real world. I started feeling like a normal person after about six weeks. What is normal? Normal was getting five hours of sleep a night and getting a shower daily. That is what I considered normal. Showering and sleep were HUGE in newborn land.

It was time to pull the band-aid off. I became less of a zombie and more like a human. A Mombie! I'm not sure if any mom is ever ready to go back to work. It was time for me. I was going to learn how to balance my son and work my job. The never-ending mom balancing act. My new routine with the baby was over.

I wanted to stay home with Levi. Staying home wasn't a financial option for us. Being a stay-at-home mom was not in the cards for me. Part of me wanted to get back to the adult world. I wanted a break from feedings and diapers. I wanted to be around other adults. I wanted to talk about other things besides poop and feedings. The other side of me wanted to quit my job. I never wanted to leave my son.

My thoughts were driving me crazy. What if something happened to Levi? What if he got sick? The scenarios were endless. I was spiraling out of control. Going back to work was inevitable but I wanted to delay it. I had to figure out our new normal. I had to see what life would be like for me as a working mom.

Emotionally, I was a wreck. I was not pregnant anymore, so shouldn't my crazy pregnancy hormones be gone? I was over the new mom sleep-deprived stage. I should be able to control my own emotions now. The pull between staying home with him and going back to work was nerve-wracking. Someone, please kick me out the door!

He was only six weeks old and had changed drastically. There was a chance I might miss one of his firsts. I had no choice; work was calling my name. It was time to take my first step into the working world. How was I going to survive?

I'm going to survive like all the mothers before me. I am not the first mom to face working life. I should be comforted because I am not the first. But it didn't comfort me. I had to come to terms that I might miss one of his firsts—his first word, first crawl, or first step. The amount of guilt I felt was overwhelming. Let's face it, all moms that go back to work will face the same obstacles I faced. I learned to manage my new life as a mom and a career woman.

My sister Stephanie was my childcare. Thankfully, she felt like an extension of myself. She became a lifesaver and a best friend. I'm extremely lucky that I had a family member that would take care of Levi. It was still hard to leave him. Stephanie made it a tad bit easier to go back to work.

It was an adjustment period for us all. I thought going back into the workforce would help get the old Melissa back. Old Melissa was gone. My life was completely different now. Leaving him on the first day was one of the hardest things I've ever done. I didn't want to leave him. My sister kicked me out the door. Let me review the schedule one more time and make sure Stephanie is ready. I was a complete disaster. My sister has always been a calming force for me.

Leave, Melissa!

To the career women that are reading this book, you are a great mom. You are not a bad mom if you want to have a career. You can rock as a mom and have a career. It doesn't mean that you are any less of a mom. I enjoyed my kid-free time and it helped me cherish the baby moments more. Working moms can go after a career and still be an awesome mom. Working moms have a different set of mom problems than stay-at-home moms do. They are juggling work commitments and motherhood. To all the stay-at-home moms, you're on 24/7.

> ### Disclaimer
>
> You will not stop missing your baby. Will it be easy? NO! There will be days that you want to cry your eyes out. Days that you will be glad you are at work and not at home. Days that you will feel like you suck at motherhood and your job. And if you think it gets better when they are older, you are WRONG. The juggling act between anything you do and motherhood will always be a constant battle.

Mom guilt is real. I haven't figured out some magical way to deal with the guilt. I constantly feel bad for all the things I didn't do right and never good about the ones I did do right. That statement sums up mom guilt. What helps me, is knowing that mom guilt will be a constant. You will always feel that you did something wrong or missed out on something. It's a never-ending battle. If you believe that all mothers have it figured out—you are wrong. We are all fumbling around. We all struggle with the pull between obligations and our kids.

Stepping out into the world after having your first baby will be a journey. It will be full of emotions and fatigue. You're a new mom. Be patient as you adjust to being a working mom. You will NOT flip a switch and

Fat and *Pregnant*

have it all figured out. Give yourself the time to figure it out. Don't beat yourself up if you make some mistakes along the way—you're a rookie.

You can do this!

Cheat List

Y'all, this is the cheat list you didn't know you needed. You're going to need it. Life is going to be different with a baby. Some days you will not recognize yourself. Some days you will feel like you are not in control of your life. I listed a couple of things that I hope will make your life a little bit easier. A helpful list that I wish was available when I had my first baby.

Sleep

Learn to sleep when your baby sleeps. There will be times when you will use nap time to clean your house and catch up on chores. Balance the work with the rest. Accept that you will not sleep through the night for a very long time. Naps help you survive the sleep-deprived nights. It will get better; you will become less of a mom zombie. Until then, take naps.

Boobs

Your boobs will never be the same after having a baby. Accept it. I had major trouble getting my milk to come and when it did it was too late. My boobs wouldn't stop leaking and they hurt for a couple of weeks. My nipples were killing me. I wasn't even a breastfeeding mom. My boobs never recovered from having babies.

Umbilical Cord Care

You need to keep the belly button area clean. I used alcohol and a Q-tip to clean the umbilical area. It took about two weeks for the umbilical cord to fall off. Disclaimer: It looked gross and dried up when it's about to fall off.

Help

Ask for help! It will be hard because as women we believe we can do it all. Trust me, we can try. If you do it all—you will burn out. We need to reset and rest so we can be a better momma. Motherhood teaches you the meaning of sleep deprivation and exhaustion. Accept help when people offer it. I wish I could replicate my sister for everyone, but she is all mine. I wouldn't have survived the first weeks without her in my life. She would come over and know what I needed. I wouldn't even have to ask for help. I will always be grateful for her help and company. She supported me and held me up in my dark times. Have a support system and take advantage when they offer it. If anyone wants to mom shame you for not being perfect, don't answer the door.

Bleeding

You will bleed for a long time. I hope you enjoyed the period-free months because it's over. After delivery, you will have vaginal postpartum bleeding. It was the worst period of my life. Who needs the medical terminology? My bleeding lasted forever. For two weeks, I thought I would never stop bleeding. I rocked the granny panties and monster pads the entire time. My new best friend was the Always purple pads. I didn't even know pads this size existed until I had a baby. I had to wear two pads and sleep on bed pads at night. It was not pretty. It got worse before it got better. Be prepared for accidents. Eventually, it will stop. Remember, you had a nine-month break. Payback isn't fun.

Emotional Monster

You will be an emotional monster. You will not be in control of your emotions. My uncontrolled emotions were the direct result of sleep deprivation, physical, and mental changes. I thought it would end once I delivered my son. Instead, my emotions were worse than when I was pregnant. I would go from crying to yelling. This was my new norm for a while. Your family and friends should understand that you're a new mom. Emotions come with the new mom package.

Schedule

It will come. Do not rush to get on a schedule. For the first few weeks focus on surviving the exhaustion. Focus on yourself and the baby. Nothing else. You will figure out the schedule. Perfection doesn't exist in motherhood. So, don't listen to the mom bloggers that stress the schedule. Embrace your child and a schedule that works for you and your baby.

Google

Google LESS. Google can be your best friend and your worst enemy. If you search for your symptoms, it comes up with two million results. Before you know it, you believe you're dying from an incurable disease. Googling can quickly escalate your stress level as a new mom. Be careful when Googling baby symptoms, but use what your read with discretion and good judgment. For example, when your child doesn't chew a chip up and it gets stuck. Google told me to lay her flat on the ground and drink coke. What finally went down her throat? The chip. At times, Google can be extremely helpful.

Pictures

Take lots of pictures. They grow fast. In the first year, they will change, and you will regret it if you don't have pictures. I have a baby book to keep all the pictures together. Is the baby book finished? No, the baby book isn't finished. I keep on saying one day I will finish Levi's baby book. I have all the material, but I keep on procrastinating. New Mom Story: We were getting newborn pictures which ended up being about two weeks after he was born. We got awesome newborn pictures. Once we were done with the last picture, Levi peed everywhere. Since Levi was naked for the pictures, Josh got drenched with Levi's urine. It was a great memory and the pictures turned out perfect.

Trust Yourself

Everyone will want to give you unsolicited advice. Moms have the best advice. Sometimes what worked for them might not work for your baby. Remember to trust your gut. Your inner mom intuition will be your guide.

The Chapter of Firsts

So, I wanted to share some heartwarming memories and some of the bad memories. Most of the memories make me feel warm and fuzzy. Some of the stories make me cringe. A lot of your first memories will be gross, full of tears, and lots of laughter. From the first time I got squirted in the face with urine, projectile vomit, first shots—buckle up! Ladies, I'm going to share some of my top-secret memories.

First Bath

Yes, I had the baby bathtub, baby soap, and washcloths. Did I know how to clean my baby? No. I was worried about hurting him or hitting his head. Stephanie stepped up and gave him his first bath. She took over and showed me how to give him a bath. I felt like I was going to hurt him. Had she ever bathed a baby? No. Why was I so nervous? I'm not sure. He enjoyed bath time. Best part? The clean baby smell.

Growth Spurts

Your baby will have growth spurts. The growth spurts are not on a set schedule. I learned about growth spurts the hard way. This memory is a hard one and makes me feel like a crappy mom. I didn't know that as my child grew, I would need to increase his formula amount. It's a very basic concept that I didn't know. Levi was about three weeks old and we were finally getting out of the house. We took him to visit Grandma's and it was a horrible first visit. We figured a short visit would be a good test run. He had been cranky for about two days and I couldn't figure out why. He started crying and wouldn't stop. I used the "3's of Baby" and it wasn't working. He was fed, burped, and had a clean diaper. I couldn't get him to stop crying. What was wrong with him? I was at a breaking point. I was doubting my abilities as a mom, a title that I've only had for three weeks. I should know what my son needs.

I was in full crazy mom mode and now I was crying with my baby. Then my friend casually said, "He's probably having a growth spurt and needs more formula." Could it really be that simple? I thought if I fed him too much, he would get fat. I didn't want to make him fat like me. Yes, I know this is probably the stupidest thing any mom could say. I didn't know that the formula would increase as he grew. Sure enough, I made another bottle and he stopped crying.

He was hungry, that was the solution. Did I win the Worst Mom Award? This memory is one of the main reasons I wrote this book. I wanted to share my entire journey. It wasn't all rainbows and butterflies. I share it because I know my story will help another mom. A mom like me. A mom that didn't know about babies. A mom that got pregnant while she was fat. My son couldn't tell me what he needed. I had to learn to pay attention to his cues or the process of elimination. This was one of the most embarrassing moments of my life as a mom. I was a newbie. One day your child will be able to talk and tell you what they need. Then you will be wishing they would be quiet.

Projectile Vomit

It will happen. I want to say to be prepared to be covered in vomit. Disclaimer: We were new parents. We received unsolicited advice and it didn't work out as planned. A friend suggested that we put rice cereal in his bottle at bedtime. It would make his belly fuller so he would sleep through the night. I believed it was the solution for me to get uninterrupted sleep. We tried and quickly regretted this parenting decision. About twenty minutes after drinking the formula and cereal mix, the all-night vomit fest began.

At first, it started off with crying. The cereal was hurting his stomach. Once the vomit started it felt like it would never stop. I was crying as much as my son was crying. All I could do was hold and comfort him. I let him throw up on me until it was done. It was on my hair, clothes, and the floor. I wish I could make him feel better. What surprised me the most? Is how far a baby can vomit. How can such a small body produce so much vomit? Mom lesson: Be careful what advice you take from other people. It might not be the best option for you and your baby. Trust your instincts, it will guide you down the right path. The cereal might work great for other moms, but not for this one.

Teething

Teething is fun . . . said no mother, ever. When you see those pretty white teeth pop through, you're thrilled. Your baby's grin is extra cute. It's cute for you but painful for the baby. The first tooth is a huge milestone. Levi's first tooth came in without much of a fuss. The rest were not as easy. Teething would make him extremely fussy and he would chew on everything. What made teething worse? The pain made him unable to sleep through the night. All you can do is soothe your baby. The only thing that seemed to ease his pain was a cold teething ring.

First Words

Levi took his time to speak and now he doesn't stop talking. He made a lot of noises but no words. When he finally said his first words it melted my heart. There was a battle between me and my better half if Mom or Dad would be his first word. I won! I had just sat him in his Pack'n Play. I accidentally shut the light off and it went completely dark in the room. Then I heard, "Mama." The sweetest words I have ever heard.

First Night Away

There will come a time when you will get a baby-free night. I wasn't ready to leave him with someone else. Melissa needed a night off. My sister offered to give us a night off. We got to be Melissa and Josh. It's been so long, and I felt guilty the entire time. I couldn't pass a baby-free night. I was still adjusting to being a working mom. I was ready to sleep and be Melissa for a couple of hours. Was it hard? Yes. Was it something that this new momma needed? Yes. Did I worry all night? Yes. I had to let my guilt and fears go. Does it make me a bad mom? No! All moms need a break.

First Birthday

The first birthday was the best. The first of many birthdays that bring your families together to celebrate your child getting older. I couldn't wait to sing Happy Birthday and watch him smash the cake. It was even better than I imagined it could be. This day was marked by another huge milestone. His first steps. Levi had been walking with assistance or with his Mickey Mouse walker. Once he saw his cousin walking it was game on. His cousin was about a year older than him. Levi was off walking after his cousin. The days of needing help to walk were over.

There will be a lot of firsts. Cherish the good and bad ones first. The first fever will be followed by your baby recovering. They grow fast and you will look back wondering where the time went. It seems hard during the rough times but a blur when recalling all the memories.

Cherish the baby time. Soon it will be toddler time followed by school time. Followed by teen years where they hate you. When they are little, you are the center of their world. Cherish it!

Get Your Body Back

What does get your body back mean? I had to discuss this because it's different for big mommas. At least it was different for me. I was overweight before I got pregnant. I still felt like I had to get my body back. This concept was strange to me since I lost weight during most of my pregnancy.

My get your body back thoughts were different than a skinny girl's thoughts would be. I was worried about gaining the weight back that I had lost. I enjoyed being pregnant because it controlled my weight. Pregnancy prevented me from overeating. Now that I wasn't pregnant, I didn't have the pregnancy roadblock. I could eat what I wanted. I didn't have to stop. It didn't make me feel bad to overeat.

The nine months I was pregnant, my eating was controlled by the baby. Now I was having to decide what I should eat. I would make bad choices. What was different this time? I was aware of my bad eating habits. Awareness didn't change my eating habits. I realized that I didn't physically need to eat all this junk. I however went back to my old habits.

I was faced with the reality that I could make better choices. The lifetime of bad habits was preventing me from making good choices. How do I change a lifetime of bad habits? I let all my old habits come back—and the old Melissa was back. I realized I was an emotional eater. What did I have a lot of after having a baby? Emotions. I felt like I was spiraling because I couldn't control myself. All the new mom emotions and guilt added to sleep deprivation made me use eating as my coping mechanism. The struggle to get my body back backfired. It made my body image issues worse.

I began struggling with my control over my weight. Would I ever be able to change? How was I supposed to tackle my eating issues and a newborn? I didn't even try to be different. I continued to do what was comfortable. I didn't binge eat, but I would eat more than I did when I was pregnant. Even though I was aware of it, I would ignore it.

My body was different since I had my son. It looked and felt different. My stomach still poked out more than before. It didn't shrink. The biggest difference was my boobs. I hoped they would go back to normal. The only way I would get normal boobs again was with the help of a plastic surgeon. Until then, I fell in love with my deflated boobs.

The only advice I would give you would be to focus on you and your baby. Listen to your doctors' directions on how and when to work on your body. Give yourself time to heal before you start worrying about losing the baby weight. You are responsible for another human being. They are incapable of taking care of themselves and need you at your best. If you are ready to work on your body, go get it sister!

I believe the most important aspect is to figure out your life as a mom. The average maternity leave is about six weeks. It took me the entire six weeks to find any resemblance to my old self. I wish I cherished the moments more instead of focusing on fixing a battle that I've had my entire life. There will be a time to start focusing on getting healthier and losing the weight you gained.

If you are reading this book it's because you are part of the big girl club. Or you are a mom that wants to read every book you can on motherhood. No matter what size you are, I hope you read this book and keep an open mind. Whenever you decide to start working on your pre-baby body or if you want to focus on other adventures—make sure you do what works best for you.

Try to be patient with yourself. We will always be our worst critics. Social media doesn't help with our self-image. Many times, you will see celebrity moms that have bounced back in six weeks. It's an unrealistic expectation that we believe is a reality. Normal moms do not have celebrity trainers and chefs making our meals. We are eating granola bars and iced lattes from Starbucks. Own it, ladies! Don't believe the pictures you see online—it's not real life!

You rock the stretchy yoga pants and bun life. Live your best life. Don't focus on the number on the scale but rather the quality of your life as a new mom. Save the scale watching days for another day. There will be a time to work on your body. When you are ready—you will make the time.

The End is Here!

We made it to the end! Thank you for reading my pregnancy story and guidebook. I never thought that when I got pregnant my story was going to be completely different than everyone else. Different from what I was taught as normal. My childhood wasn't normal. My adult life wasn't normal. Why would my pregnancy be normal? Yes, I'm different and I'm okay with being different. I have never been the skinny girl. I will never be labeled as a skinny girl. I was overweight when I got pregnant and overweight when I delivered my son.

From the beginning, I was worried about my pregnancy being doomed. The statistics were against my pregnancy. The doctors reminded me that my odds were low of having an "easy" pregnancy and delivery. The mixture of my fears and the doctors' so-called science data—made me an emotional wreck my entire pregnancy. I could never just be pregnant because I knew something could go wrong at any moment. I had zero security in my pregnancy.

My pregnancy and delivery was a wild ride. It changed me—for the better. I am grateful that I have the label of Mom. I hope from reading my story that you will learn to love yourself a little bit more. Pregnancy is never easy. Pregnancy as a fat girl will be different from your skinny friends.

I felt inadequate in my pregnancy because of my weight. I struggled with believing that I could give my baby a fair shot at life. I wasn't even sure

Fat and Pregnant

if I could get him to the delivery room. I understand that every pregnancy is different. Any woman can have complications during their pregnancy. For us big girls there is more of a chance for something to go wrong. Will you be the last fat and pregnant girl? No! Was I the first pregnant fat girl? No. Being fat and pregnant, your journey will be an uphill battle. I believe we big mommas have a difficult battle.

Hope. There is hope. My story proves there is hope for big girls. I have no clue how your pregnancy will go. I hope my story gives you hope when it feels like the world is against you. When all the people ask why you didn't wait to get pregnant until you've lost weight. Why didn't you get healthy first? When you wonder if you can even survive being pregnant. When you feel that you don't measure up to other pregnant women because you are fat. Hope—it does exist in the big girl tribe. You are a warrior in this tribe. It doesn't matter if this is your first pregnancy or your fourth. We are in this together!

You are fat and pregnant.

Beautifully, big and pregnant.

Plus size and pregnant.

Fluffy and pregnant.

Awesomely pregnant.

Whatever you want to call your pregnancy. You are worth it! My story began when I became a fat and pregnant girl...

www.ingramcontent.com/pod-product-compliance
Lightning Source LLC
Chambersburg PA
CBHW070926080526
44589CB00013B/1441